ADVANCE PRAISE FOR
The Rib Joint: A Memoir in Essays

"Julia Koets's collection of essays, *The Rib Joint*, is a marvel of form and content: this dazzling writer has created a guidebook for growing up queer in the American South. Told with honesty, humor, and pathos, each of these essays is a testament to human endurance and dignity. Oh, how lucky we all are to have this book in the world."

—Nick White, author of *How to Survive a Summer*

"'If a girl grows up in a small town,' writes Julia Koets in one of many haunting fragments from her nonfiction debut, *The Rib Joint*. 'No one hears of girls falling for girls there.' Or we didn't—not often— until now. I love poets like Koets who turn to memoir to plumb their histories, who enrich the fourth genre with elegant rhythms, relentless inspections of language, and images that smolder long after the page is turned. I love this book for all these reasons, so tender, incisive, and pulsing with truth that it seems to have a heartbeat all its own."

—Julie Marie Wade, author of *Wishbone: A Memoir in Fractures*, Winner of the Lambda Literary Award

"Julia Koets's debut memoir, *The Rib Joint*, is as intellectually capacious as it is emotionally charged. Although these essays read as stand-alone stars, the full force of the book is in its constellation

of vivi⟨   and

Greek   lesire

express   rical,

urgent   ⟩ss of

essentialist philosophies about the dynamics of love, and a deep awareness of the intersections of self and place. Yet, her luminous imagery and beautifully wrought colloquial cadences create a style of abundance. This is a work that is grounded in the particular but resonates out and out, as Koets herself tells us in the book's titular essay: 'Narratives of queerness are infinite. They do not always begin at birth. They cannot always be traced to childhood. A story can begin in medias res, as a wave begins in the middle of the ocean.'"

—Danielle Deulen, author of *The Riots*

"In this powerful and urgent memoir, Julia Koets shifts artfully between narrative modes—confessional, axiomatic, lyrical, metaphorical, scholarly. The formal restlessness generates both feeling and meaning, and it is a most compelling way to convey the author's struggle for identity."

—Chris Bachelder, author of *The Throwback Special*, National Book Award Finalist

The Rib Joint

a memoir
in essays

Julia Koets

2017
Red Hen Press
NONFICTION
AWARD

 Red Hen Press | *Pasadena, CA*

AUTHOR'S NOTE: The names and certain identifying characteristics of some people in my life have been changed to protect their anonymity.

Library of Congress Cataloging-in-Publication Data

Names: Koets, Julia, author.
Title: The rib joint : a memoir in essays / Julia Koets.
Description: First edition. | Pasadena : Red Hen Press, [2019] | 2017 Red Hen Press Nonfiction Award
Identifiers: LCCN 2019033844 (print) | LCCN 2019033845 (ebook) | ISBN 9781597096751 (trade paperback) | ISBN 9781597098410 (ebook)
Subjects: LCSH: Koets, Julia. | Women authors, American—20th century—Biography.
Classification: LCC PS3611.O38 Z46 2019 (print) | LCC PS3611.O38 (ebook) | DDC 813/.6 [B]—dc23
LC record available at https://lccn.loc.gov/2019033844

The National Endowment for the Arts, the Los Angeles County Arts Commission, the Ahmanson Foundation, the Dwight Stuart Youth Fund, the Max Factor Family Foundation, the Pasadena Tournament of Roses Foundation, the Pasadena Arts & Culture Commission and the City of Pasadena Cultural Affairs Division, the City of Los Angeles Department of Cultural Affairs, the Audrey & Sydney Irmas Charitable Foundation, the Kinder Morgan Foundation, the Meta & George Rosenberg Foundation, the Allergan Foundation, the Riordan Foundation, Amazon Literary Partnership, and the Mara W. Breech Foundation partially support Red Hen Press.

First Edition
Published by Red Hen Press
www.redhen.org

ACKNOWLEDGMENTS

Thank you to Mark Doty for selecting *The Rib Joint* for the 2017 Red Hen Press Nonfiction Book Award, and to Mark and Kate and all of the staff at Red Hen Press for their support and generosity.

Thank you to all of my teachers and mentors for their kindness and support, especially Danielle Deulen, Christine Mok, John Drury, and Kristen Iversen, who all read sections of this book in various stages. Thank you to Rachel Toliver, for her sharp and invaluable edits and comments, for helping me make this book better.

Thank you to all the friends who supported me and provided me with thoughtful feedback during the writing of this book, especially those in the creative writing program at the University of Cincinnati: Linwood Rumney, Sarah Rose Nordgren, Rochelle Hurt, Lisa Summe, Anne Valente, Sara Watson, and Dan Groves.

Thank you to Hannah Godwin, whose company during garden walks helped sustain me as I worked on the final edits of this book. Thank you to Kelly Blewett, for taking walks in cemeteries and for always asking me what I'm thinking about. Thank you to Jacqui Simmons Groves, for reading countless drafts of this book, and for always knowing the right questions to ask.

Thank you to the people who trusted me with these stories. Thank you to the girl who taught me how to drive stick-shift in her Volkswagen Rabbit. Thank you to the girl who taught me how to eat a pomegranate. Thank you to the girl who loved the linden trees. Thank you to the girl who taught me about bioluminescence. Thank you to the girl who walked with me everywhere during our childhood. Thank you to the girl who left something in Barbados and who taught me how to talk more openly.

Thank you to Lindsey, for writing back when I wrote, "What do you teach?"

Thank you to my brother for growing up right beside me. And thank you, most of all, to my parents—for planting an azalea when I was born and for telling me it was okay to doubt.

for my grandmother, Julia Stinson Pharr,
who showed me how to float on my back in the ocean
and how to write a good letter

CONTENTS

Astronomy of the Closet: Seven Axioms   13

Variations on Drive   25

When Pandora Was a Myth   29

Azalea   37

The Rib Joint   48

Variations on Falling   69

How to Ignite   74

Limbo   82

Fire House   89

Variations on Praise   96

The Organ   98

Spectrum   106

Variations on Moor   113

Blood Money   117

Variations on Grit   122

How to Leave   125

The Rib Joint

ASTRONOMY OF THE CLOSET:
SEVEN AXIOMS

... [E]ven people who share all or most of our own positionings along these crude axes [of family, love, work, play, etc.] may still be different enough from us, and from each other, to seem like all but different species.
—Eve Sedgwick, *Epistemology of the Closet*

On June 18, 1983, nearly three months after I was born, NASA's seventh space shuttle mission departed from Kennedy Space Center in Cape Canaveral, Florida. On board was Sally Ride, the first American woman in space.

Ride came out publicly, for the first time, in her obituary on July 23, 2012. It's a strange proposition: coming out of the closet from the grave. It wasn't a loud coming-out; if you didn't read the obituary closely enough or all the way through to the end, you could miss it. In the Space & Cosmos section of the *New York Times*, reporter Denise Grady noted in paragraph forty-two of Ride's obituary, "Dr. Ride is survived by her partner of 27 years, Tam O'Shaughnessy."

A week before Ride died of pancreatic cancer, she and Tam talked about how the obituary would address their relationship. Remembering that conversation, a little over a year after Ride's death, Tam spoke with Human Rights Campaign writer Maureen McCarty and said, "It was [during our discussion about Sally's obituary] that I realized no one knows who I am."

Axiom 1: Fear can affect the body in much the same way as gravitational pressure. We can implode. We can disappear.

In third grade, my class created a solar system. We unrolled heavy rolls of black paper on the blue carpeted floor and cut large sections of the paper with our dull, red-handled classroom scissors. We cut the black sheets unevenly, hard as we tried to follow a straight line, to be perfect. The edges were ragged and torn in places where our scissors lost all sharpness. It didn't matter, though. No one focused on the imperfections. We lined the off-white cinderblock class-room walls, the dusty vinyl ceiling tiles, and the rectangular ceil-ing lights with the black paper we'd cut. We made papier-mâché planets with rings and moons, covered them with glow-in-the-dark paint, and hung them from the ceiling with fishing line. We cov-ered the windows with cardboard and then lined them with black paper, too, making sure no light could get into our room. Our teacher, Mrs. Dantzler, called it The Black Hole.

It wasn't scientifically accurate, but I liked the way it sounded. We learned that you can never come out of a real black hole in outer space. The gravitational pull is so strong there that even the small-est particle of light remains inside indefinitely. My class construct-ed outer space in that room, and we lived in there from 8:00 a.m. to 3:00 p.m., with a break for lunch and recess. We must have studied other subjects, practiced our multiplication tables, learned the U.S. presidents, but all I remember of that year is The Black Hole.

When we turned off all of the classroom lights, our bodies glowed with specks of luminescent paint, the way E.T.'s finger glowed when he pointed towards *home*. In my attic bedroom at home I stuck glow-in-the-dark stars on the slanted ceiling to rep-licate the experience. When I laid down to fall asleep at night, I stared up at the fluorescent stars, glad that I could reach my hand up and touch them if I wanted, that I could prove to myself, again and again, that things could exist in the dark.

I didn't have a hard childhood. I grew up in a middle-class house-hold on a tree-lined street in a small town in South Carolina. In elementary school, I walked or rode my bike to school with my three best friends. After school, we biked to the pharmacy in the old town square to buy five-cent bubble gum and fountain cokes. We strolled through the aisles of the yellow pet shop on the corner, seeing how much the cane toad had grown in his aquarium tank since our last visit a few days before. I didn't get picked on in school. My friends were the kind I could trust. In our backyard my parents built my brother and me a tree house out of salvaged wood. I took a can of red paint from the shed, and my best friend Laura and I dipped our hands inside, up to our wrists. We pressed our red palms on the inside boards of the tree house, so no one would forget us.

Sometimes, though, I felt a void inside me. The space started in my throat when I didn't voice what I was thinking. When I knew that I *couldn't* voice what I was thinking. The void moved down into my trachea, my lungs, my gallbladder until stars started to form in my tissues, my veins. I was glowing with fear. I could only let myself think of a girl I liked, let my thoughts land on her, when no one else was around. I knew in the pit of my bones that when "Sweet Caroline" came on the radio in my mom's Jeep Cherokee I should feel ashamed for thinking about a girl I knew.

Growing up, I sat next to my mom on our small, screened-in back porch after school and told her about my day, what we'd done in art class, a fight I'd had with my best friend, my doubts about religion.

"Doubt isn't a bad thing," she always told me.

But I didn't tell my mom that I might be gay. I thought that if I said the words out loud, I might never be able to take them back. So I learned how to live in a void until my blood pressure became atmospheric, until my body shook and I couldn't breathe.

Axiom 2: Danger is implicit in queer theory, as it is in astronomy.

Recall the early debates around astronomy and religion: the helio-centric theory, the Roman Catholic Inquisition of 1633, Galileo's imprisonment.

In my early twenties, I went on a family trip with the girl I was secretly dating. Sarah's aunt and uncle got a deal on a hotel suite at a beachfront hotel in Florida because they agreed to listen to a three-hour presentation on timeshares. One night, while we were eating dinner in the hotel suite, Sarah's cousin, a hyperactive middle school boy who was already starting to grow facial hair above his upper lip, said, "Swimming with a shirt on is *so gay.*"

It wasn't that he thought the kid with the shirt on in the hotel pool that afternoon was actually gay. He just thought it was stupid to wear a shirt in a pool. Sarah's other two teenage cousins continued eating their mashed potatoes, seeming not to notice anything offensive about what he'd said. Sarah didn't normally speak up when her conservative Baptist family said offensive things, and this comment was nothing compared to other things I'd heard her family say, so I was surprised when she asked her cousin why he'd used the word "gay" to mean the same thing as *awful* or *weird.*

"Well, it *is* weird," he said. Everybody laughed except Sarah and me.

"And awful," her aunt added, lifting a forkful of chicken to her mouth.

Sarah's uncle passed the bowl of peas to one of his kid's friends. I could feel the tension building like a presence, like it took a seat at the head of the table.

"What if one of your own kids was gay?" Sarah asked her aunt.

I was glad and anxious at the same time. I was relieved Sarah was speaking up, but I didn't know if I could handle her aunt's answer, not now, not in Florida, hundreds of miles from home, not in this cramped hotel suite where I would be spending the rest of the week.

I waited. I wanted to see Sarah's aunt really think about the question, to watch it for a minute, like the millions of people who watched the Space Shuttle Columbia, the first flight of NASA's Space Shuttle program, take off from the landing pad at Cape Canaveral in 1981. I wanted to see her eyes widen as the question challenged everything she knew about God and sin, the way people crowded around the glow of their television sets to see people leave the atmosphere and orbit Earth in outer space.

I wanted Sarah's aunt to imagine the *people* inside the question, like the first astronauts ever to try orbiting Earth inside a shuttle.

"I'd give him a gun," she said.

Axiom 3: We must study fear so we can name it when we see it.

In an interview with *BuzzFeed News* reporter Chris Geidner on July 23, 2012, Sally Ride's sister, Bear, said, "I hope it makes it easier for kids growing up gay that they know that another one of their heroes was like them."

When I first read Sally Ride's obituary, I questioned why she'd waited so long to come out. I thought of all the lives she could have affected by coming out when she was still alive, how my own life might have been different if I'd been able to see her not only as an astronaut, but as a lesbian. But then I thought, no, she didn't have to come out to the whole world. She told her close friends and her family, and that was enough.

I wasn't born in the 1950s. I wasn't eighteen during the Stonewall Riots. I wasn't twenty-six when Anita Bryant began the "Save Our Children" campaign. I wasn't the daughter of two elders in the Presbyterian Church. I didn't study nonlinear optics. The whole world didn't watch me shatter the atmosphere in a space shuttle aimed at so much darkness.

In her interview with the Human Rights Campaign, Tam said,

"It's scary to be open [about your sexuality] because you don't realize the impact that it might have on so many aspects of your life [. . .] You worry about grants, about whether you'll be able to continue writing children's textbooks; we were scared that if sponsors knew the founders of Sally Ride Science were two lesbians, [it] would affect our organization."

Coming out is not a one-time act. We come out to every new friend, every new colleague, every new neighbor, every new acquaintance. I don't want to come out and come out and come out. I am often afraid to come out. But I was fourteen when Kenneth Brewer tried to kiss Stephen Bright, and Bright beat him to death. I was twenty-three when someone stabbed Ryan Keith Skipper twenty times, slit his throat, and left him to die on a dark, rural road in Wahneta, Florida. I'm thirty-two and Indiana recently passed the Religious Freedom Restoration Act, condoning discrimination against gay, lesbian, and transgender people. I have been scared. I have not always come out. I have often longed for outer space.

In an interview with *Harvard Business Review*'s Senior Editor Alison Beard, conducted shortly before Ride's death, Beard asked Sally Ride why she'd said she'd never wanted to be a hero. Ride responded, "I never went into physics or the astronaut corps to become a role model. But after my first flight it became clear to me that I was one. And I began to understand the importance of that to people. [. . .] You can't be what you can't see."

Axiom 4: Erasure is an act of theft, a carrying off with.

When Sarah married a man several years ago, she invited me to the ceremony. Lindsey, my girlfriend of several years whom Sarah had met the summer before, wasn't invited. Lindsey and I decided to drive nine hours south from Ohio for the wedding, because the price of gas was less expensive than a flight. When I went to the wedding that Saturday afternoon, Lindsey ordered a pizza to be delivered to our hotel room.

I didn't know whether my girlfriend's exclusion was on purpose or whether it was a matter of numbers, the cost of dinner plates at the reception. I wondered whether Sarah's fiancé considered my relationship with Lindsey unnatural, something God didn't intend. Sarah told her husband about her relationship with me when they first started dating eight months earlier. She sent me an e-mail several days after their conversation and told me how well it went, that he hadn't run or kicked her out of his house like she thought he might, that he said, "It doesn't surprise me about Julia, and I think there is forgiveness for that."

Sitting in a pew near the back of the church on Sarah's wedding day, I watched other people take their seats. It was strange, I thought, that no one knew who I was. I was anonymous among the faces filling up the rows. For all they knew, I could have known Sarah from the church she attended as a child. I knew all of the Bible verses, the hymns, the rituals. I, too, grew up inside a church, albeit a less conservative church than Sarah's.

I felt out of place and realized that I'd sat on the wrong side of the church. I'd been in such a hurry to find a seat, to not draw attention to the fact that I was there alone, that I didn't think to ask which side was the bride's. I would have been just as out of place on Sarah's side, though. Some part of me felt erased, like the sun during an eclipse, still there, but obscured. Sarah's aunt and uncle and cousins, the ones we'd vacationed with in Florida, sat near the front of the other side of the church. Sarah's cousin, that middle school boy who'd had hair on his upper lip, now had a full beard. Sarah's aunt was talking to someone in the row behind her. She was smiling so big that I thought her face might break into bright flames.

In his homily, the priest spoke of marriage as a covenant between one man and one woman. Nearly everyone laughed when he made a joke about the church being the bride of Christ. He didn't like the idea of being Jesus's bride, he said. In other words, he wanted the congregation to know he did not like to think about marrying a man, about being feminine, about wearing a dress.

I didn't stay long at the reception. I didn't see the first dance or try to catch the yellow daisy bouquet. I found a couple that I knew through Sarah and sat with them while I ate baked beans and cornbread from the barbeque buffet. I hadn't seen them in over seven years. They had one kid and another on the way. When they asked what I'd been up to since I'd seen them last, I avoided telling them that I was living with a woman, that we'd moved across the country together to start a PhD program in literature in Ohio.

I didn't want to hear them stumble for the right words to say in response. My relationship with my girlfriend wasn't a secret. Either of them could have looked at the pictures on my Facebook page and easily figured it out, but I didn't want to have to come out to them. I didn't know if I could trust them with it. They were driving back home that night to be with their son. I was glad to drive back to the hotel a few miles away and eat a slice of cold pizza in bed next to my girlfriend.

Axiom 5: Though certain narratives erase the fact of queerness, queerness does not simply disappear.

When Sarah posted her wedding pictures on Facebook a few months later, I scrolled through them. I zoomed in on her face in a few of the photographs, trying to figure out if she was happy. Sarah always hid her feelings better than I, so I knew her happiness would be hard to gauge. She buried things, where not even she could see them. Years ago, it had taken eight months and many conversations for her to admit that she had more-than-friends feelings for me.

I hoped she was happy, that a man made her happy. When Sarah and I dated in secret, kissing only in the darkest of rooms where no one else could see us, we talked about coming out together. She'd said that if she came out, she wanted to know that we were going to get married, that she was making this decision knowing we would be together forever. I couldn't do it. I'd only dated two women (both in secret) and I didn't think I could even call it dating because things don't have the same names when no one knows about them.

When you date in secret, the pressure is different. You're weightless. You're stuck in between jumping and landing. You exist in midair. Your bones start to thin. You hover over every threshold.

I scrolled to a picture near the end of the wedding album. The groomsmen had decorated Sarah's husband's car for the couple's send-off at the end of the night. They'd tied a string of soda cans to the exhaust pipe, taped white balloons to both sides of the car, handcuffed a black ball and chain to the steering wheel, and written a message on the back window. I felt my face flush with anger when I read it. At the way it erased me from Sarah's past, voiding our relationship as if it'd never happened. *Honk / Just Married / Virgins on Board.*

When Sarah and her husband walked outside hand-in-hand through the middle of everyone, when Sarah hugged her mom, when she and her new husband drove slowly away, the tin cans rattling against the road, the people in the crowd must have cheered.

Axiom 6: We can be several places at once.

There is a photograph of Sally Ride in outer space where her skin glows brightly in a strange window light. She doesn't look scared or hesitant. She looks at peace. She's looking down at Earth.

"When I was orbiting Earth in the space shuttle," Sally said, "I could float over to a window and gaze down [. . .] I could see the coral reefs in the oceans, fertile farmlands in the valleys [. . .] Even from space, it is obvious that Earth is a living planet."

Sally could be two places at the same time. She was at home in outer space and on Earth with Tam and the people she loved. I imagine a bird fluttering inside her chest—undisclosed, but bright.

Axiom 7: To welcome is to want.

On a recent drive to visit my parents in South Carolina with Lindsey, we stopped at the UFO Welcome Center in Bowman, about forty miles north of where I grew up in Summerville. This exit was familiar to me, but I'd never seen the UFO. I didn't know the UFO Welcome Center existed until a year ago. Anytime my family took a trip north of home and passed the Bowman exit on Interstate 26, my parents would say, "Positive!" My brother and I started saying it, too, on subsequent trips. For as long as I can remember, I've said "Positive!" whenever we've passed by Bowman.

"That's where we stopped and used a pay phone to call the doctor," my mom said the first time she yelled "Positive!" as we drove past the Bowman exit.

I was five, maybe younger. I sat in the backseat of our family's Honda station wagon next to my little brother.

Lindsey and I got off at the Bowman exit and drove toward town, past rusted silos, dilapidated trailers, and fields orange with flowering weeds. The town looked abandoned when we reached it. Shops and houses sat boarded up, forgotten. We wondered where everyone went and how long they'd been gone. When we got out of the car, we could hear the metal siding of the saucer-shaped UFO flapping in the wind. Spray-painted black across the middle of the ship: *UFO Welcome Center.*

No one was around. The mobile home behind the ship was quiet. The roof of the UFO was pieced together with strips of shiny tin, fiberglass, and old wood. I could tell that it took time and patience to build. Jody Pendarvis must have scoured trash piles, dumps, and abandoned houses in Bowman for years to collect the materials he needed. He began construction in 1994, he told field reviewers for Roadside America, "Your Online Guide to Off-Beat Tourist Attractions."

Pendarvis planned for his UFO "to be a place where aliens could be comfortable meeting people from Earth (it's 46 feet across, the same diameter as most UFOs, according to Jody [Pendarvis]). He later added a second, smaller saucer on top so that the aliens can take Jody with them when they leave." Only eight screws hold together the entire structure, Pendarvis told the field reviewer. The second saucer just balances on top of the lower one, so that it can levitate easily into space.

Spray-painted on metal siding in Pendarvis's yard, the gangway door to the inside of the ship warns: *SPACE PEOPLE ONLY. UNSAFE. ENTER AT YOUR OWN RISK. NO EARTH PEOPLE.* I pushed the door open and walked toward the hull of the ship to get a closer look.

Lindsey walked our two dogs around the other side of the ship.

"There's a rocket behind that fence," I heard her yell, as the dogs sniffed the tufts of uncut grass.

A string of multicolored Christmas lights hung, unlit, from the warped boards of the ship's walls. I could see inside the ship through the holes where boards had at some point slipped: a toilet, wooden steps up to the second saucer, power outlets, plastic chairs. Piles of trash lined the ground at the base of the UFO: a white elementary school chair, two rusted red lawn mowers, a queen-size mattress, broken cinder blocks, ancient computer monitors, paint cans, a moldy van seat, AC units, boxy televisions.

The Roadside America website I pulled up on my cell phone listed Pendarvis's phone number as the contact for a tour of the inside. When I called, the operator said the number had been disconnected. A table saw stood mid-cut in front of me, as if Pendarvis had just vanished, leaving a pile of yellow sawdust behind.

"We found out that we were pregnant with you right there!" my mom said, as she pointed toward a dense patch of pine trees in the distance, as if to say, *Right there, that's where you came down to Earth.*

VARIATIONS ON DRIVE

I was sixteen, a sophomore in high school, and she was in college, six years older. When she taught me how to drive stick-shift, was this a literal iteration of *sex drive*?

I drove an automatic burgundy 1985 Ford LTD station wagon, a car my parents got for free from my dad's aunt. *The Period,* my brother and his friends called it, because every inch of the car—the bumper, the doors, the cloth seats, the dash, the radio dials—was a deep red, the color of menstrual blood.

I was dating a guy at my high school who drove a black Chevrolet Camaro. He washed and waxed it every Saturday, until it shone like a betsy beetle.

I liked the way my boyfriend's legs looked when he leaned over the top of his car to clean the roof and when he played basketball. When he drove to the basket, his lean leg muscles flexed. He was tall enough to dunk.

I also liked how easily the college girl I had a crush on drove her black Volkswagen Rabbit. She let the clutch out slowly, gave the engine just the right amount of gas. She didn't care that the car was old, that it needed some work. She wore her blonde hair pulled back in a ponytail, and she smelled like oranges.

So he wouldn't have to drive The Period, my brother practiced driving my parents' manual Jeep Cherokee. I practiced, too, in our church's gravel parking lot.

Prayer could be considered a kind of drive, a persistence, a vigorous working towards a particular objective: prayer for the sick to be healed, prayer for forgiveness from sin, prayer for no other cars in the lot, no youth minister checking the oil in the church van, no kids at the basketball hoop, no one to see my parents' Jeep lurch forward and stall with me at the wheel.

In her parents' driveway, the girl I had a crush on showed me the order of the gears on the shifter of her Volkswagen. Sitting in the driver's seat, I tried to memorize the gear pattern on the black knob. She put her hand on top of my hand and we shifted together, moving from first to second to third.

"When you start the car, you need to have it in neutral," she said, her hand still on mine, as she showed me how easily the shifter moved from side to side in neutral.

For years, I played at prayer with a concentrated momentum. One night, I prayed for this girl to be gay. I explained to God that I wanted to kiss this girl, and the only way it seemed possible was if she was gay.

"Can you hear that," she asked me, as we drove the back streets of her neighborhood, "the way the engine sounds right there?"

I listened to the engine rev like a swarm of bees, pushed in the clutch pedal, and moved the gearshift into third.

Her Volkswagen shifted with an ease that my parents' Jeep lacked. It was more difficult to stall out in her car, I realized, as I downshifted and stopped at a busy intersection.

"Turn right here," she said, not hesitating to take me out onto a busy road.

That December I helped my mom carry her heavy camera equipment and adjust the lights at the city's annual debutante ball, which she'd been hired to photograph. The girl I had a crush on was there in a long, red dress. She wasn't a debutante, but some of her close friends were. Taking a break to get a glass of water, I saw her dancing with a guy in the ballroom under chandelier light.

Neither the girl I had a crush on nor I could imagine the lives that we'd be living in ten years. She'll be married to a woman, and I'll be secretly dating a woman.

She'll come out when I'm in college, and I'll watch how people we know react to the news. I'll study the faces of people at our church. I'll notice if they call her relationship a sin. I'll learn who not to come out to when I come out a few years after her.

But when I was sixteen, on a night when a group of girls in bridal-white dresses and pearly, elbow-length gloves came out to society as women of a certain age, I drank a glass of cold water at the edge of the dance floor and wondered who was leading whom, who was driving whom across the shiny, low-lit dance floor, the girl-I-had-a-crush-on's steps in sync with a man's.

I held the gearstick tightly with my right hand as I drove, even when I didn't need to shift gears. The girl I had a crush on sat calmly in the passenger seat. I worried that in my inexperience I might be doing something wrong, that I might be stripping her gears as I shifted, but she wasn't worried.

"You're doing great," she said.

WHEN PANDORA WAS A MYTH

The bright lights above our neighborhood pool emitted a low electric pulse through the night air. I lay on my stomach in a floral print bathing suit, propped up on my elbows to search the boom box radio for a good song. The green carpet of the pool shelter floor made my skin itch, but at the end of May the nights were already balmy in the Lowcountry of South Carolina, and the cool slab of concrete under the carpet felt good against my skin.

My brother turned ten that week, two years younger than I. Alone next to the wooden picnic tables, where my mom had tied a few balloons and started a line of streamers from the roof beams earlier in the afternoon, I could hear my brother and his friends playing another round of Sharks and Minnows in the deep end. It was getting late and soon parents would come to pick up their sons.

I moved the radio tuning bar slowly across the numbers so I wouldn't miss a station in the pool of static.

This was 1995. Pandora was still a myth. You had to be patient to find the song you wanted. Patient, from the French *pacient*: capable of enduring pain without complaint. It's a word that shares its root with *pati*: passion, from the Ancient Greek πῆμα: suffering.

I endlessly rewound and fast-forwarded tapes on my Walkman, and I didn't own many albums—my parents said they were too expensive. As a compromise, my dad bought me a four-pack of blank tapes wrapped in crinkly plastic. I recorded songs from the radio, taping over them when I ran out of room: The Cranberries "Linger"; Salt-N-Pepa "Whatta Man"; US3 "Cantaloop (Flip Fantasia)"; Toni Braxton "Breathe Again"; Ace of Base "The Sign."

Some nights I spent hours making a mix tape. I wanted to record each song in full, so if I tuned into a station to find that a song I wanted had already begun, even if it was just seconds in, I waited until it came on again.

The Greek Pandora myth is a creation story, one about the first human woman on Earth. In this creation story, the first woman opened a jar instead of a piece of fruit, releasing every sin into the world. In one version of the Pandora myth, instead of containing every evil, the jar contained blessings, which would have been preserved had Pandora not given into curiosity and opened the jar. Pandora, a name meaning both *all gifts* and *all-giving*. Both versions of the story blame a woman for the existence of sin, and both versions changed in the sixteenth century when a scholar mistranslated *pithos*, meaning *jar*, to *pyxis*, meaning *box*. With this mistake, Pandora's jar became Pandora's box.

Desire didn't make sense in middle school. I had crushes on boys, and while those were easy to recognize and okay to talk about, even they were confusing.

One of my best friends' parents owned a photography business, and they took all the pictures for the city youth football league. I was in sixth grade, and my friend's mom made me a cut-out magnet from a photograph she took of a boy I had a crush on; in his red jersey, tight football pants, and uniform padding, his small shoulders and thighs looked more muscular, more like the older boys my friends and I found on folded posters in the teen magazines at the CVS downtown. We rode our bikes there just to see the pictures. We sat cross-legged in the blue-carpeted aisle and flipped through new issues of all the teen magazines, not having the money to buy anything.

I hung the magnet of my crush inside my locker at school. Thankfully, my crush never saw it because we only "went out" for thirty minutes one day.

I don't think I knew back then that I had crushes on girls, too.

In sixth grade, the only things I knew about lesbians were that they were adults who wore baggy cargo shorts, cut their hair like boys, and played soccer. I didn't do any of those things. Sure, I played one season of soccer when I was eight, but I quit because it was a co-ed league and the boys rarely passed the ball to any of the girls on our team.

I certainly didn't know anything about bisexuality or that sexuality exists on a spectrum. And I was only twelve, still a girl, and girls couldn't be lesbians, I thought. *Lesbian* was something that a few people mysteriously became when they grew up, the way some people became astronauts.

My first real kiss, one that I didn't get practicing with my best friends or playing truth or dare, was with a boy.

While my parents wouldn't spend money on cassette albums for my music collection, they did invest in cotillion. Growing up in the South, etiquette and propriety were almost as important as being able to read or multiply fractions.

At middle school cotillion the girls wore dresses, curtsied, and learned how to dance properly with boys. I took cotillion lessons in my church's parish hall on Tuesday afternoons in sixth grade, and the first time I saw Steven dancing the foxtrot in his suit and tie, I knew I wanted to kiss him. His hands were sweaty the first time we danced the shag, which made me thankful that all the girls had to wear white gloves. We switched partners in a big circle and I counted the number of boys I had to dance with until I got to dance with Steven again.

Mrs. Whipple—this is her real name—made her way around the circle adjusting our arms and backs, correcting our posture.

"Stand up straight. Let's try that again," she said and started the song over on her record player.

We step-ball-stepped and step-ball-stepped across the slick laminate floor to B.J. Thomas' "Rain Drops Keep Falling on My Head."

We didn't know what to do with our bodies. We didn't know how to fit inside them or how to move. Like a pandora, a type of marine mollusk, we were both shell and body, both inside and out. *Mollusk,* from the Greek, from Aristotle's *ta malaká,* the soft things. Girls who started developing breasts early hunched their backs a little to try to keep anyone from noticing. Some boys' arms grew faster than their soft torsos or legs, like gangly insects.

Steven and I kissed in Azalea Park that spring of sixth grade, two months before my brother's birthday party. My friend Jessica slept over, and when she and I snuck down to the park after dark to meet Steven, the fluorescent lights over the tennis courts hummed in anticipation.

Steven laid his red bike down in the grass and sat next to me on the wooden bench that faced the pond where my friends and I caught tadpoles. Steven turned his baseball cap around backwards so the bill of it wouldn't get in the way.

Hundreds of frogs croaked and croaked. Like that red pouch that bloomed under a lizard's neck to attract a possible mate, the azaleas on the bushes seemed to be pulsating. Jessica stood in the grass and when Steven and I kissed, she took a picture with a disposable camera, the bright flash effusing the pool of dark around our small bodies.

In *Eros, the Bittersweet*, Anne Carson writes about the triangulation of desire in Sappho's fragments. When Sappho watches the woman she loves sitting with a man, she writes: "He is a god in my eyes— / the man who is allowed / to sit beside you . . . If I meet / you suddenly, I can't / speak—my tongue is broken; / a thin flame runs under / my skin."

After Steven and I kissed, I watched Jessica do back handsprings in front of us, her thin frame forming a perfect curve, like her whole body smiled in the air each time she jumped backwards. She curled over and over and over until she said she was dizzy. I felt dizzy just watching her.

That was the other confusing thing about desire: it came, and then it moved on to someone else so quickly that it was hard to study.

Jessica's birthday pool party was the same night as my brother's that year, and I begged my mom for weeks to let me go.

"None of my friends will be at Joseph's party," I pleaded. "I've gone to his birthday for nine years. He won't care if I don't go just this once."

I didn't tell my mom, "I have to go." I didn't say, "I love Jessica. I'll never get this chance again."

I wonder if I knew somewhere in my twelve-year-old subconscious that I felt something more than friendship for Jessica. I wouldn't or couldn't admit it then, though, even if I had recognized it that way.

A hazy line can exist between friendship and desire, but I

didn't see the possibility for haziness then. I couldn't. I didn't know desire could look that way. With the exception of my aunt, who lived hundreds of miles away from our small Southern town, I didn't know any lesbians, and at that point I didn't know my aunt dated women. I didn't know same-sex desire was possible, not really, not in the way I knew that girls liked boys until infinity, and that girls and boys got older and taller and married and had children and it started all over again.

When Bryan Adams' "Have You Ever Really Loved a Woman" came on the boom box radio the night of my brother and Jessica's birthday pool parties, I wished I had one of my tapes with me to record it. I could smell the chlorine on my skin as I lay there by myself on the pool shelter floor. It was the first time I'd ever heard the song, and I wanted to listen to it over and over again. I wanted to remember all the song's imperatives.

Desire was like the deep end of the pool at night. I couldn't always distinguish where the water ended below me. "In Greek lyric poetry, eros is an experience of melting," Anne Carson writes. "The god of desire himself is traditionally called 'melter of limbs.'" Treading water, my legs and arms started to feel like they were melting, becoming part of the water all around me. My limbs turned to rubber; the water played tricks on my eyes. I imagined a shark coming up from the bottom of the deep end—its sleek, grey body becoming visible right at that hazy line between the cement floor and the uncertain depths below.

When I listened to Bryan Adams in the corner of the pool shelter, the air was charged with something close to fear—because I didn't want anyone to catch me. I thought they might see right through me, that they'd know why I liked the song. I worried my body was completely water, and my desire glimmered under the surface of my skin, like one of the brightly-colored dive rings my friends and I tossed into the deep end and saw gleaming near the center drain.

I turned down the volume on the boom box. I dove to the bottom of myself to retrieve my heart before anyone else saw it so exposed.

In music period in the spring of sixth grade, our class learned how to play Bette Midler's "Wind Beneath My Wings" on our off-white plastic recorders. We sat up straight in our laminate desks and did our best to remember which holes to cover as the song played from a tape in our teacher's boom box.

We always seemed to be a little off-key, and when someone hit a particularly wrong note, which happened more frequently than not, the high-pitched noise made me squint, as if I could shut out the noise if I shut my eyes.

I listened to the lyrics and focused on moving my fingers at the right moment. Heroes flew to the moon and did the right thing; they were the people on our classroom posters: Michael Jordan, Amelia Earhart, Martin Luther King, Jr. In this song the person she was singing about seemed more personal than a hero, though. This woman was telling someone else a secret. Someone she knew really well. She loved this person. It wasn't quite a love song, though. Heroes weren't girlfriends or boyfriends. Having a hero didn't mean you were in love. There was nothing dangerous or forbidden about having a hero, I thought. If anything, heroes were what our teachers and parents expected us to have, the way they expected all the girls to fall in love with the boys and all the boys to fall in love with the girls.

I planned to write Jessica a note that I'd pass to her in the hall-way between classes: "Did you ever know that you're my hero?"

But I never gave it to her. Maybe I knew that it would be too revealing. Maybe somewhere in the back of my mind I knew that it was a strange and dangerous thing to tell her, for a girl to tell any girl. Or maybe I lost the note in my backpack, the small, torn-out piece of notebook paper hidden between the pages of my math book.

One night that sixth-grade year, I wrote the initials of the boys I had crushes on inside the earphone compartment of my pink and turquoise P'Jammer AM/FM alarm clock radio:

J.R.
P.Y.
W.M.
T.D.

While, on some level, I didn't know that I had crushes on girls in middle school, too, it was important that I left proof of my crushes on boys.

I might've thought, subconsciously, that if anyone suspected that I had secrets and went looking for them, they wouldn't look any further than what was written, somewhat covertly, inside the little door of my boxy clock radio. They'd open it, find a secret and be satisfied, a gift rewarding their curiosity.

AZALEA

When my best friend Laura and I were nine, we spent an afternoon making a box. No, we spent an afternoon trying to make a box disappear. Into something that would not be noticed. Into something that would not be seen by anyone other than the two of us. We dripped white globs of glue on small pieces of paper we'd cut into rectangles. Our fingers stuck together when we pressed azalea leaves and petals on the top, the bottom, on all the sides of the box. At the edge of Saint John the Beloved's property line, the halfway point between our two houses, Laura and I balanced the box we'd made in the branches of a large, pink azalea bush.

We left notes there for each other. They had to be short enough to fold and fit into the small box we'd made. Think about the size of a tooth. Our handwriting had to be thin. Think of the tiny gap between my two front teeth. The box was no wider than our wrists.

When it started to get warmer, we had to be careful not to disturb the bees. It was a game, like double-riding on our bicycles—one of us steadying herself on the handlebars, steering both of us with her hips.

The year I was born, my parents planted an azalea bush beside our dirt driveway. Pale pink blooms, the color of my skin when my father bathed me, minutes after the doctors handed me to him. In the warm water I finally stopped crying, opened my dark brown eyes, and looked up at him, he told me years later. My mother told me my eyes looked just like hers.

That morning in March, snow dusted the pine trees in Flowertown. My father had not yet built or painted the white picket fence. Our small front yard looked bare, the dirt too sandy to grow iris, primrose, gardenia, or hydrangea. Each year, the azaleas were the only plants that never died, that always came back. A pink balloon tied to the porch banister of our house bumped into one of the wooden columns holding up the tin red roof: *It's a Girl!*

In Chinese culture, the azalea symbolizes softness, temperance, womanhood.

In elementary school Laura and I gave our dolls communion, breaking apart pieces of white sandwich bread.

"Here," we told them, placing a small piece of bread on the floor in front of each doll. "Take, eat: This is my Body, given for you."

Within a fourth of a mile of our two houses, there were seven churches, including the one Laura's family and mine attended, where her father was the priest. Every Wednesday Laura and I walked with our friends to choir practice. Every Sunday we went to the weekly service and Sunday school. During Lent, we ate vegetable soup and peanut butter sandwiches in the church hall on Wednesday nights. On other afternoons we rode our bikes across the church grounds, making up stories about the people buried in the hundred-year-old graves. Laura and I knew the church as well as we knew each other's bodies—the California-shaped scar on my right knee, the tapered thinness of Laura's fingers, the circumference of each other's ponytails.

When we were not at church or in school, Laura and I lived in each other's houses. Our mothers disciplined us like we were both their daughters. One night my father cooked us okra, boiled the frozen ladies' fingers in a pot. The seeds, slimy in our mouths, slid down our tiny throats.

My mother placed azaleas from the bush my parents planted on every pink-icing birthday cake she made for me. She carefully pulled out the pistils and stamens with the calyx, splayed the bloom open, and put a candle in the center of each azalea.

When Laura and I kissed, we were still girls, and it was a game. We were twelve and stayed up late talking in her twin bed. In order to fit in her bed, we had to lie closely, like notes in a small box.

I asked her if she wanted to tongue wrestle, like thumb wrestling, like I knew I would win. But when her tongue was suddenly in my mouth, I realized I'd never played this game before. I realized how unsteady my tongue was, how my body started to shake. I was scared of what kissing her meant, of what kissing any girl meant. I left her room and went into the bathroom, thinking I might throw up. When I came back, I lay down on the floor, in a bed of pillows and blankets her mom had made for me.

"Yes, everything is okay," I told Laura.

My teeth chattered so hard in my mouth I thought they might break and shatter into hundreds of pieces.

In Turkish folk medicine, the leaves of azaleas, of rhododendrons, relieve inflammation, reduce rheumatic pain, cure a toothache, reduce anxiety.

In the boxy white church van on the drive back from a middle school youth group scavenger hunt, I asked one of the chaperones, a woman who had recently joined our church, why she'd said some sins aren't forgivable, why she'd said being gay means you're going to hell. I don't remember how the conversation turned in that direction, but I remember that she wasn't talking about me directly, so I felt safe questioning her.

"Well, the reason homosexuals are going to hell," she said, "isn't because they're homosexuals. It's because they act on their desires."

Before that day I'd never heard anyone at my church say homosexuality was a sin. I don't remember anyone ever talking about it. Even though I didn't believe what she said, couldn't believe what she said, I'd never been afraid of dying until then.

Azalea ingestion in dogs can result in drooling, loss of appetite, leg paralysis, coma, or death. A horticulturist at Louisiana State University recalls a time someone left a puppy alone in the house with a potted azalea. The puppy didn't survive.

Years after my parents planted my azalea, the branches sprawled and scratched my brother's and my arms if we forgot to swerve away from them when we biked up the driveway after school. Every March, my azaleas opened, petals as soft and thin as skin peeling from a blister.

"Azalea is the number one must-have plant in the South," says *Southern Living*. "Growing 8 to 12 feet tall and wide, it smothers itself in spring."

The first day of my freshman year of college, I sat beside a girl in math class.

"I'm Kate," she said.

Kate's parents were both priests, like Laura's father.

Some nights Kate and I stayed up so late talking that our eyes lost their ability to perceive depth. I reached out my arm to measure how far away she was from me. She pushed a strand of her blonde hair behind one ear. Leaning our backs against the wall, we let our legs hang off the edge of her dorm room twin bed. Then, turning toward me, she tucked her painted red toes under my thigh to keep them warm.

Her boyfriend lived two states away, and I didn't know how he stood it, how he measured the distance each night. My boyfriend lived two hours away, a distance I'd started to feel less and less.

Red azalea on the cliff, [. . .] / Whose intimacy embraces distance. / You remind us of our first love.

Drunk one night the fall of our junior year, both of us single, Kate told me I better take this chance. Better kiss her. Better take off her shirt. Better unclasp her bra. Better unbutton her jeans.

"This won't happen again," she said.

Better lift up my arms. Better let her take off my shirt. Better slip off my jeans. Better let her kiss me. Better let her kiss me again. This won't happen again. Better kiss her again. This won't happen again. This won't happen again. And again.

Kate asked me to go to a Bible study with a few of our friends.

"Small Group," she said.

We met in the ministry leader's living room: books stood neatly on her shelves; the brick fireplace was painted a crisp white; picture frames said *family* and *faith*. We sat in a circle of chairs and read passages the leader had picked for that night. I don't remember any of the specific words, but at the end of the first meeting the leader started to pray and somewhere in the middle of it she said, "and we pray for those people struggling with homosexual desires."

Walking back that night to our dorm after the meeting, Kate assured me that the prayer wasn't referring to me: "How would she even know?"

Somewhere in the dark, I knew Kate hadn't told anyone I thought I might be gay, but I also knew keeping my sexuality a secret wasn't about protecting me. She was protecting herself.

August of our junior year, when the heat was sharp enough to hurt you, a boy came back from summer break with a new body, a few fading acne scars pocking his newly taut jawline. I hadn't seen him coming. When Kate and I saw him running shirtless across the intramural field behind our dorms that first week of classes, I thought he was a transfer student. He hadn't even existed at our small college, it seemed, until that moment. He'd been there the whole time, of course, for two years, with acne and husky jeans.

Spring of our junior year, he took Kate home, if a dorm room counts as home. She took him home, too, if a dorm room counts as home. I'd realize later, months after Kate started dating him, that he'd sat one row over from me in our small freshman literature class two years earlier.

"Brian," he'd said, when he'd introduced himself to me and Kate.

In Chinese mythology, the King of Shu fled his kingdom in shame after a forbidden love affair. The king turned into a cuckoo bird and sang ceaselessly in spring until he spit blood onto the ground beneath him. From his blood, azaleas bloomed.

Home for the summer, I sat with my mom in her car, which smelled faintly of cinnamon chewing gum and the lipstick she used to blush her cheeks. It was no one's birthday, but chocolate ice cream dripped down my mom's sugar cone. She licked it before it ran down her hand. Before we drove home, she said she wanted to ask me something. I felt the ice cream curdle a little in my stomach. I'd been anticipating this conversation, hoping I could avoid it a little longer.

"Are you struggling with your sexuality?" she asked.

I swallowed until I started to cry.

"Mad Honey," made from azalea nectar, has been reported to cause cardiac arrhythmia, emesis, mild paralysis, and convulsions in humans.

On the hot concrete path to my parent's front porch, I sat in the sun with my knees pulled up to my chest. I didn't get up when I heard the screen door open and my dad walk out. I didn't turn around to look at him when he put his hand on my shoulder and told me he loved me. I didn't say anything as he went up the stairs to go back inside. I knew my mom had just told him about the conversation we'd had in the car, how my tears had said more than any words could. I sat there until I could get up. Until I knew I wouldn't start to cry again.

Unlike dogs and cats, when rabbits ingest azaleas, they cannot throw up.

My mom asked me if I would be okay with her talking to a priest at our church, to talk through how she was feeling after I told her that I might be gay.

"That's fine," I told her reluctantly, a bit unsure whether I wanted anyone at our church to know.

"I love you no matter what," she said, "but I'm worried. Things are going to be harder for you."

The next time Kate and I kissed we moved a flimsy twin mattress onto the floor. It had been more than two years. We'd graduated from college.

She was still dating Brian but they were doing long-distance. She and I were backpacking around Greece and Italy for a month; that night we were on the island of Corfu. At The Pink Palace, a youth hostel right on the water, everything was pink: the walls, the bus to the ferry, the booze cruise sailboat, the balcony attached to our room. Every night was a party, but Kate and I went back to our room after dinner one night.

I'd told myself after she'd left me for Brian that I wouldn't kiss her ever again. But that night our skin hummed with so much want.

"Sit here," she said, and I did. "Put your hands here," she said, and I did.

As I sat in the only chair in the room—a wooden desk chair with slats in the back—she tied my hands behind my back with the spaghetti-strap tank top she'd worn earlier that day.

"Don't move," she said.

And I didn't.

The summer after my first year of graduate school, Kate and I visited Laura and her boyfriend in California. We were both single. Kate had been sleeping with a guy from home, but they weren't together, she said.

In San Francisco, people in costumes crowded the streets for the Bay to Breakers race. Kate and Laura were the only people I knew in the city, so I felt anonymous—and bold from the tequila and beer—and tried to hold Kate's hand somewhere in the mess of people walking along the Panhandle. Kate pulled her hand away, as if to remind me, we must keep this a secret—what we did in rooms like little boxes no one could see inside.

In my late-twenties, when I moved to San Francisco after graduate school, I got a job at an elementary school in Chinatown. In celebration of Chinese New Year that first year, two third-graders asked me what year I was born.

"1983," I told them, smiling at their eagerness.

"Are you as old as my mom," one of them asked, and I laughed, as the other one quickly turned to a page in a classroom book about the Chinese zodiac animals.

They smiled and, using a finger to guide them through a paragraph, they read me what the book said about people born in 1983: "The year of the boar. You are the twelfth and last zodiac sign. Your natural element is water. You are intuitive, born sensitive and seeking beauty. You took a long time to cross the river." In Chinese culture, the azalea is known as "the thinking of home bush." I thought of the miles between me and where I'd for so long called home.

Late on the night I flew home to South Carolina for Christmas, I lay down on my childhood bed and opened my laptop to check my e-mail. I clicked on a link my mom had sent me to the most recent blog entry the priest at my childhood church had written on the church's website. I read the words of the priest who coached my church basketball team in high school, who'd told me I had one of the sweetest shots he'd ever seen. I read how he didn't believe that LGBTQ parishioners should have leadership roles in the church. He said he disagreed with the Episcopal Church's recently revised, more progressive canons about sexuality and gender expression: "Yes, all people are welcomed at Christ's table and into his family ... But, this revised canon goes further to say that individuals who struggle with their sexual identity and who express themselves by cross-dressing, etc., are, nevertheless, to be seen as eligible and qualified to be ordained, to be hired to staff or elected to vestry leadership."

I'd planned to go to the Christmas Eve service with my family the next day, but now I wondered if I had come out in middle school or high school, would I have been allowed to be an acolyte, a small group leader at youth group, a voice in the choir? He said "all people are welcomed at Christ's table" at our church, that communion includes people like me, but his words felt hollow, like a box without anything inside.

It was mid-March in San Francisco when my mom called early in the morning from South Carolina to wish me a happy twenty-eighth birthday.

"Your azaleas have started to bloom," she said.

Like a dusting of snow the morning I was born, pollen covered my parents' front porch. I pictured my mom standing in her worn red slippers on the old pine floor of the little house where I grew up. I knew the angle to which the sun was cutting across the kitchen floor.

"The whole town is glowing," she said.

Pink, fuchsia, white, and coral azaleas covered the churchyards, the old town square, the white picket fences, the sides of every road. Down the street from that little green house with the red roof, over two hundred thousand people flooded Azalea Park and Main Street for the annual three-day Flowertown Festival to celebrate the town's "most flamboyant season."

In floriography, the language of flowers, azalea means "Take care of yourself for me." When the mail arrived at my apartment later that day, I opened a birthday card from my parents. A pressed pink azalea fell out of the envelope as I opened it.

THE RIB JOINT

The body knows / when something large has shifted: it accumulates / loss in hidden places—joints, crevices, between bone—until / suddenly recognition hits and manifests itself: / the body, parallel to the earth, convulsing like a wave.

—Jennifer S. Cheng, "Anthropology of the Body [2.1]"

An octopus protects itself by hiding in plain sight. Lacking both an internal and external skeleton, and with thousands of pigment-changing cells just below the surface of its skin, in disguise, it can change not only its color but also its texture and shape. An octopus can blend in with almost anything: rough head of coral, spiny polyp cluster, tunicate-ridden side of a sunken ship.

As two University of California, Berkeley biologists discovered, one species of octopus disguises itself by wrapping its six arms around its body and walking backwards on its two legs. Another octopus "coils its two front arms and raises them in a pose that somewhat resembles algae." Without a rib cage to protect its three hearts, one particular species known as the "mimic octopus" can shapeshift into a sea snake, flounder, or lionfish.

I disguised myself for years. I hid in plain sight. In college, my best friend, Kate, and I slept together in a small twin bed, as if inside a jar—it didn't seem possible that we could both fit so comfortably. We locked the door to her bedroom, as if sealing a lid, making sure no one could get inside.

Unlike the octopus, curiously able to open and escape a sealed container, I could not imagine such openness. I could not imagine coming out. Not in the South. Not at nineteen.

Kate and I met during the first week of college. The afternoon of the first day of classes, I sat nervously in a small classroom, waiting for the math professor to arrive. I smiled when Kate walked past me and chose the seat behind mine. I'd seen her in my dorm the first night after I'd moved in, but we hadn't officially met. I noticed how pretty she was—her shoulder-length blonde hair, her long neck, her peacock-green eyes.

Maybe we went to lunch after class that day, or maybe we studied for the first test together later that week, or maybe we ran into each other in a dorm hallway. The truth is, I can't remember exactly where it happened, but it wasn't long before Kate and I were always together, joined at the hip.

To escape our small Southern college town, Kate and I drove. We left our quiet campus late at night in the blue 1990 Oldsmobile sedan I had inherited from my grandmother. Some nights, we didn't pass a single car on the road. All that seemed to exist out there were pine trees.

Our college had fewer than 1,300 students, and almost everyone lived in the dorms and ate their meals in the one cafeteria on campus. I looked forward to the nights in the car with Kate, when everyone we knew was several tiny towns away. We could have been driving nowhere, and some nights we *did* drive nowhere—we just drove until we turned around. The car was one of the only places where Kate and I could talk without anyone else hearing; what we said seemed safe inside my midnight blue sedan. Our thin bodies relaxed into the blue cloth seats. Kate propped her bare feet on the blue dashboard, her toes pressed against the windshield. I wrapped my hands around the blue steering wheel and adjusted the blue radio dial to find a good song. We both complained that only country songs came on within a thirty-mile radius of our school.

One night, I told Kate about how I had kissed my best friend in middle school.

"It's not that strange," she said as I concentrated on the dimly lit road. "Lots of girls have crushes on their best friend. I don't think it means you're a lesbian."

I was relieved. I also wondered whether Kate meant that I shouldn't worry about the ambiguity surrounding our own friendship. I wondered if she felt the ambiguity between us, too. Kate moved closer to the blue center console and rested her head against my shoulder.

"I'm getting tired," she said.

I imagined driving through thousands more towns just like that, with her head on my shoulder and some country song on the radio. Every store would be closed. Every field would be empty. Every house would be dark.

On Valentine's Day, a boy invited Kate and me—both of us—to be his dates. Maybe he couldn't decide between us, or maybe he couldn't imagine us apart.

When we got ready that night, Kate helped me put on makeup, leaned in close to line my eyes black, to brush on mascara.

"Relax your mouth," she said, as she drew on red lipstick.

She bit her bottom lip as she concentrated on my face. She folded a tissue in half and handed it to me.

"Now, do this," she told me, pressing her lips together—making a popping noise when she opened them—to show me how to blot.

Posing for a photograph later in the night, Kate and I stood in front of a taxidermied bison on display at the front of the restaurant. In the next photo, our date smiled in the middle of us, one of his arms around each of our waists. A joint in the body is where two bones come together, fasten, marry.

In an airport years later, I will see a bison skeleton on display in the middle of a wide terminal hallway. The animal's expansive ribs form an empty space that I will consider climbing into, as if the ribs are the ropes of a hammock, a structure encouraging me to rest inside it for a while.

Hundreds of peacock feathers covered Kate's parents' yard in a suburb of Tampa, Florida. The iridescent blue and green birds roosted on people's roofs all over the neighborhood. I didn't know a bird so large could fly that high, lifting itself twenty or thirty feet into the air. I'd never seen anything like it. The giant birds were everywhere—perched in an expansive oak tree, walking the grass path to the back patio, crossing the street out front. Down the center rib of one tail feather that'd fallen in the street by my car, a gold eyespot glinted in the sun. And like the peacock feathers changing between blue and green without warning, Kate's eyes were green and also blue.

I drove down from South Carolina to Florida to visit Kate during the summer. At night in her queen bed we heard the large, bright birds land on the roof. Lying next to each other, we listened to one peacock cry on the balcony outside Kate's second floor window.

"It sounds like it's saying one word over and over," I said quietly, "but I can't quite tell what word it is."

A few years before, when my godmother fell off the top rung of an eight-foot ladder and broke the head of her humerus, the long bone in the upper arm between the elbow joint and the shoulder, her husband mistook her high-pitched cries for the neighbor's peacock.

"Johhhnnnn! Johhhnnnn! Johhhnnnn!," she cried for fifteen minutes before he realized it was her and not the bird.

Sophomore year, we lived in the same dorm, and one night that fall, Kate crawled into my skinny bottom bunk. Our skin was still warm from summer. Her back against my chest, she put my arm around her so that my hand rested against her ribs. With my fingers I studied the way one of her lower ribs stuck out further than the others.

We were best friends—we knew that—but we didn't talk about how the borders of our bodies had started to blur. In Classical Latin, *costa* meant "rib," which, later, in Medieval Latin, came to mean "edge" or "coast," the side of a stretch of land. We were walking the edge of a boundary neither of us would name. That night, her body slept against mine like the Atlantic against the Carolina coast.

"I want you to kiss me," Kate said one night in the spring. When she moved closer, her face so near to my face I could feel her breath, I turned away. I couldn't stop my body from shaking.

My fear of my own desire could be measured like a chemical formula, each aspect of my anxiety a letter in a chemical compound. Think of each line connecting hydrogen to carbon as a rib: a butane structure for fear. I was afraid that if I kissed Kate, the atoms inside me would split, and I might not be able to put them back in place.

I worried that my relationship with Kate would change irrevocably if we kissed. What if Kate only wanted to kiss me as an experiment, the way girls in movies joked about having experimented with a girl in college, as if the experience was so inconsequential, so minor they could laugh it off? I hated those girls, the crisp certainty of their laughs. And anyway, I didn't think they could call something an experiment if they already knew the answer to the question they were asking—they'd end up with a guy.

In the Bible, when the serpent convinced Eve to eat the fruit from the tree at the center of the garden, maybe it was the structure of the snake's body—made of so many ribs—that made her trust him. The rib was Eve's beginning, after all, her connection to God and the only other person who existed on Earth.

Maybe, at the moment when the snake told Eve she wouldn't die if she ate the forbidden fruit, she imagined her body as beautifully protected. How wonderful to fall, she thought, feeling her lungs fill and empty beneath her ribs.

We finally kissed in the fall of our junior year. I was shaking, but when Kate slid her tongue into my mouth, I forgot how scared I was. Her face was softer than any boy's I'd kissed—which was an aspect of kissing her that I hadn't considered.

The top seven sets of ribs in a human body are called true ribs because they're attached to the sternum. The lower five sets are known as false ribs because they don't directly attach to the sternum. In a very small number of genetic cases, the fourth or fifth rib of a person will not attach to the sternum in utero, making that rib neither true nor false.

The first time Kate and I kissed, I realized that everything I'd known about kissing up until then was somehow false. When Kate and I kissed, it felt like my first kiss, even though I'd kissed plenty of guys and one other girl before that night. Kate took off her shirt, shimmied out of her jeans, and crawled next to me in my twin bed.

Kissing Kate, all my nerve endings woke up—a million bees' wings, humming under the surface of my skin.

"Take off your shirt," Kate said. "This is the only time this is going to happen, so we shouldn't stop."

I knew if I told even our closest friends that I was in love with Kate, they'd think it was a sin, or at least they'd think it was objection-

able. At our college, almost everyone went to church, regardless of
how much they drank the night before or who they'd slept with.
On Sundays after morning services, the school cafeteria filled with
students in their Sunday best.

After church on Sundays, as I carried my tray of fried chick-
en, green beans, and sweet tea to my table to sit with Kate and
my friends in our college cafeteria, I sometimes worried everyone
could see right through me, that my sin was so strong you could see
it, like the outline of my body through my thin cotton dress.

That fall, Kate and I hardly got any sleep. I was never more tired
and never more awake. Kate told me that sleeping with me didn't
mean she was a lesbian.

"It doesn't mean I'm bisexual either," she said one afternoon on
one of our drives.

Miles from campus, we came upon a farm on a back road, where
we decided to stop. When we got out of the car, I noticed a herd of
strange animals running toward us from a distance, their necks tall
and alert. As the animals got closer, I realized what they were, but
the realization didn't ease my fear. I worried they were going to
jump the thin wire fence that separated us from them, that Kate
and I were going to die right there in the middle of nowhere in a
llama stampede.

"Get back in the car!" I yelled to Kate.

"It's OK," she said, laughing and moving closer to the fence.
"They aren't going to hurt us."

On the drive back to campus, after we'd stopped laughing, I
told her that naming what we were doing didn't matter—that it
didn't mean we had to stop. And we didn't.

In the spring of our junior year, a guy took Kate to a Disney on

Ice performance. After the date, lying next to me in bed, Kate told me, "We have to stop doing whatever it is we've been doing." I lay there silently.

"It's just that if I'm going to date Brian, we have to stop," she said.

The white cinderblock walls in the room glowed faintly in the dark.

"Say something," she said.

But my voice was stuck in my chest, in the tight space between my lungs and my heart.

Sarah was a biology major and a Baptist, so I began our friendship by asking her to explain things to me, as she did in the laboratory on campus: how does water run up a mountain, why do only our fingers and toes prune after swimming for hours, how can people at your church not believe in evolution?

I didn't tell Kate I had a crush on Sarah, because I wanted to keep it safe. But my reasoning was more complicated than that, if I'm being honest. When Kate continued seeing Brian after the Disney on Ice date, I felt betrayed in a way I'd never felt betrayed by anyone before, and I wanted Kate to feel what it was like to be replaced.

The two lowermost ribs of the human ribcage are called floating ribs because they don't attach, directly or indirectly, to the sternum. They have no anchor in the front of the body. When Kate started dating Brian, my whole body felt that way—detached.

I suddenly understood, more viscerally than I had before, why people call the end of a relationship *a breakup*. Why people want *a clean break*. A clean break means it's more likely that the recovery time will be shorter, that the bone will heal with less chance of infection or complications.

When Kate started dating Brian, we didn't make a clean break, the way a straight couple would do if one person started sleeping with someone else. I didn't tell her how hurt I was. I didn't tell her to end things with Brian, to choose me. I just stopped being her best friend—because that felt like the only thing I could do without completely falling apart.

On the day Eve was born, did Adam tell her God made her from one of his ribs? And, hearing this, did she trace her fingers over his chest, searching for a scar?

The summer after our junior year, I volunteered to drive with Sarah to California, to the coastal town where she was going to live with a high school friend for the summer. She'd have a free place to stay and a job waiting tables at a seafood restaurant with a view of the Pacific Ocean.

We drove from one coast to the other in four days. We took turns driving all through the first night, and by the next afternoon, we had made it from South Carolina to Albuquerque, New Mexico. We camped the rest of the nights in deserts.

We didn't expect it to get so cold at night in May. The days were hot and left us parched, but at night, the temperature dropped into the forties, and the cold air seeped through our thin nylon tent and into our bones. The first night we camped, we zipped our sleeping bags together to conserve heat, and when that wasn't enough, we moved as close to each other as we could. I put my arm around Sarah's waist. When I got back from the trip, Kate asked if anything was going on between Sarah and me. She was still dating Brian—he'd mailed her a letter every day of summer break. Nothing had happened between Sarah and me on the trip, not technically. We'd never kissed or talked about the undercurrent between us.

"No," I answered Kate over the phone, "but I don't know why you'd care."

"We're supposed to be best friends," she said.

That's the problem with sleeping with your best friend. I didn't realize until then that I wasn't sure whether Kate and I had ever been just friends. Had I loved her from the first night of college, the first time I saw her in my dorm? From the moment I saw her walk into that math class? From the night she taught me how to blot my lips? From the night she rested her head on my shoulder in my car?

The first time Sarah and I kissed, more than halfway through our senior year, I asked her to make a scientific hypothesis: "how many times can I kiss you before you kiss me on the mouth?"

Lying next to her in bed, on her dark blue sheets, I ran my hand under her T-shirt and across her stomach.

I kissed her forearm—*one*. Her skin was warm in the middle of February.

Two—just below the sleeve of her T-shirt.

Then an inch above her collar—*three*.

She pushed a strand of hair behind her ear.

I could feel her heart racing through her skin.

Four—a few inches higher on her neck.

She kissed me on the mouth when I looked up at her.

If you look at a map of the 1,700 islands that make up the Florida Keys, it looks like a bent spine, curving off the coast of the mainland.

For spring break our senior year Kate, Brian, Sarah, and I

camped at the KOA on the Sugarloaf Key. Kate had suggested the trip months before, and I knew it was a bad idea. We were room-mates again, but either we didn't talk at all or, when we did, we fought. I'd thought that if I said no to the trip, we'd only fight more.

It rained almost every night in the Keys. We set up one large tent for the four of us the first afternoon we arrived, and, as we cooked hot dogs on the fire in the early evening, for a few hours I thought that the trip might be good, even fun.

But when the ground flooded that night, soaking all our sleep-ing bags and clothes, Brian ran out to the shitty little beach at-tached to the campground and found two chairs. Inside the tall four-man tent, Kate and Brian slept on the long plastic lounge chairs, and Sarah and I curled up next to each other in the small back seat of her sedan, parked next to the tent. I was thankful for the privacy, for the opportunity to kiss Sarah.

The next morning, as we walked to the bathroom to brush our teeth, Kate said she needed to talk to me. Sarah gave me a knowing look and said she'd meet us back at the campsite.

Kate and I walked past the campground beach where the water curved in and the ground was covered in white rocks. Suddenly, I hated the secrecy that shrouded our relationship. I hated how Kate never wanted anyone to see us—how she'd shush me at a department store, tell me it wasn't the place to talk about certain things. I realized this wasn't fair—I'd been just as scared as she had about anyone finding out about what we talked about, about what we were doing every night—but I was mad Kate kept asking me about Sarah.

At this point it had been less than a month since Sarah and I had first kissed. Sarah didn't want me to tell anyone about what was going on between us, and I didn't fight her about it. She was scared about what it all meant. She'd never kissed a girl before. She didn't know if it was right, if she could reconcile her feelings for me with her religious beliefs. Sarah's family and her church taught her that being gay was a sin, something you might be tempted to think about but should never act on. They believed being gay could be cured with prayer, the same way some people prayed for a parking spot at Walmart.

Sarah and I argued about religion, and about her church's stance on homosexuality, but I thought telling someone about us might cause her to make a decision out of fear. I worried she might end things between us if I told anyone, including Kate. And, if I was being honest, I wasn't ready to be open about our relationship either. I was scared, too. I wasn't sure what people would say, how my friends or parents would react.

"Would you even tell me if something was going on?" Kate pushed me further.

I tossed a rock into the clear blue water.

"No," I answered.

"Do you have feelings for her?"

"Yes."

It was as honest as I thought I could be without betraying Sarah. It was also as honest as I was willing to be with Kate. And I knew this was why Kate was upset. For three years Kate and I had told each other everything. We were best friends. We'd told each other that we'd never felt more ourselves than when we were with each other. And now I wouldn't tell her about one of the most significant parts of my life.

When we graduated from college, Kate was still with Brian, and I was still secretly dating Sarah. That August, Brian was moving to North Carolina to start graduate school, and Sarah was moving to Charleston to start a job at an ecology camp. Kate suggested she and I move to Charleston together. I knew this was a bad idea, but I agreed to the plan, maybe out of guilt, maybe because I didn't want to lose Kate. If I lived in Charleston, at least I would be close to Sarah, I thought.

When Kate and I didn't know how to find the jobs we really wanted and didn't have enough money to rent a place in Charleston, we moved into the studio apartment above my mom's photography studio in my hometown, thirty miles inland, and started waitressing at a barbeque restaurant there.

"Come lick our bones," the rib joint's T-shirts said.

The one-bedroom apartment above my mom's photography studio was small but all we could afford. The roof slanted steeply down from the center of the bedroom, the small kitchen, and the thin hallway that connected the two main rooms.

The apartment was already furnished with things my mom had picked up at yard sales over the years or brought over from their house—the house I grew up in—in an effort to de-clutter. A brass twin bed with a red and white geometric quilt ran the length of one wall in the kitchen, a foot away from the small wooden table with three wobbly oak chairs. There was just enough room to pull a chair out and sit down.

In the bedroom: the metal double-bed frame, painted black to look like iron, which my parents used to have in their guest room at home with a canopy attachment. When I was twelve, my brother and I wrapped white Christmas lights around it for our newlywed seventy-five-year-old grandmother and her eighty-year-old husband when they came to visit after their wedding.

"A honeymoon bed," my ten-year-old brother and I had told them, not fully realizing the implications of the name.

Kate and I shared a bulky desktop computer that took up most of the surface space of the particleboard desk on the wall adjacent to the bed. To the left of the desk a daybed functioned as Kate's bed and our couch, which faced a built-in bookcase that held our books and the heavy TV I'd lugged back from college after graduation.

After we moved into the studio apartment, I told Kate about Sarah, even though Sarah didn't want me to tell anyone what was going on between us. But I knew I couldn't live with Kate for the next year without telling her. I wanted things to get better between us.

I eased into the words.

"Sarah and I . . ." I let the sentence out slowly, as if carefully unloosening the cap on a carbonated drink that had rolled around for months in the trunk of a car. ". . . we're together."

"How long has it been going on?" Kate asked, a tinge of anger surfacing in her voice.

The ceiling fan above the bed spun and spun, its blades inches away from the sloping walls. The window air conditioning unit rattled the glass panes.

"Nobody knows about it," I said. "She asked me not to tell anyone."

"That's not what I asked."

Like the bubbles rising in that shaken bottle of soda, I started to feel unstable, unable to control the situation.

"Since February," I said, thinking she'd already guessed as much.

"February. You've been lying to me for six months?" she asked, the question of it half-lodged in her throat. "I asked you outright months ago, and you lied to me."

When I tried to tell her how it wasn't actually a lie but a refusal to tell her, how Sarah had asked me not to tell anyone, how I thought she knew because of the way I had told her I wouldn't tell her when she'd asked, Kate lost it. She left the room, slamming the door behind her.

Before I had time to breathe, to process her reaction, the door swung back open, leaving a doorknob-size hole in the wall.

"I hate you!" she yelled. "I hate you!"

Meat is most tender closest to the bone. At the rib joint, the smell of pork fat and hickory smoke seeped into the walls, the wooden booths, the framed posters of B.B. King, the green terry cloth napkins, the dingy hardwood floors, the metal vats of sweet tea. The black rubber floor mats left a sticky, black residue on my shoulders and hands when I hosed them off with hot water and lugged them outside behind the restaurant to dry at the end of a long night shift.

It was impossible to get the smell of smoked pork out of our clothes, our shoes, our long hair pulled back in ponytails. When I dropped by my parents' house after lunch shifts, my mom started asking me to take off my work shoes before I came inside, a request she'd never made of anyone before.

Our work uniforms consisted of khaki pants, a belt, a tucked-in black T-shirt with white lettering, and all-black, non-slip shoes. I bought the cheapest pair of black shoes I could find at Payless: Grasshoppers, a brand that gave the impression that in these shoes I could leap from table to table, my slender khaki-clad legs more powerful than they appeared. The shoes, made of a thin, synthetic material meant to look like leather, made me like a grasshopper at the barbeque restaurant in only one respect: I blended in to the place, the way a bright green grasshopper blends in to a garden in the South.

I learned quickly that most customers barely noticed the wait-staff. It was as if the entire restaurant staff was a swarm of cicadas camouflaged in a southern landscape—the sounds of us stacking plates, scraping scraps into the trash, sinking dirty silverware into a half-drunk glass of sweet tea were just background noises, sounds that customers could fall asleep to on a warm summer night.

On each side of its abdomen, a cicada has a tymbal, a kind of ribcage "made of a thin membrane connecting thicker sections known as ribs, each of which is thinner than a human hair." Derke Hughes, a research engineer at the Naval Undersea Warfare Center, studied cicadas' tymbals in an attempt to discover more about how they make noise. Through a type of micro-computerized CT scan, Hughes discovered that the insects buckle out their ribs and then snap them back together, creating their unique noise.

I imagined expanding my ribs until they buckled, until their almost-breaking made a noise that in some species is considered song.

In addition to taking orders, delivering food to tables, folding baskets of silverware, and cleaning our sections at the end of a shift, the managers at the rib joint assigned side-work to each server: clean and sanitize the beverage station, restock the salad cooler, and refill the toilet paper in the bathrooms.

One night I finished my side-work early and checked with one of the managers to see if I could go home.

"I actually need you to clean the grout on the bathroom walls before you go," she told me.

You've got to be kidding me, I thought, picturing all of the tiny lines in between the squares of off-white tile. Looking back on it, she probably was kidding me on some level and wanted to see if I would call her on it. I should have told her no. I should have laughed at the ridiculousness of the request.

But, outside of the studio apartment, I avoided confrontation vehemently. My arguments with Kate were all the disagreement I could handle.

Resigned to evade conflict at all costs, I grabbed a bottle of bleach and a sponge off the supply closet shelf and started to scrub the bathroom walls.

The year Kate and I worked at the rib joint you could see my ribs. I lost weight without even realizing it. By November, my khaki work pants slid down off my hips if my belt wasn't tight enough. And my belt was never tight enough. I went from a size 6 to a size 4 to a size 2.

I had a recurring nightmare in which I was working a never-ending shift at the restaurant. The wooden booths multiplied into eternity as I looked out at my growing section of tables. Customers kept coming through the green front door. B.B. King's "Crying Won't Help You" was probably playing on repeat. I only had enough time to take down an endless list of drink orders. Infinite racks of ribs waited in the kitchen, never getting served.

"I've figured it out," another server said to me one day in February as we wrapped silverware near the end of a long lunch shift.

"What's that?" I asked, wiping a pink fleck of rib off a knife that didn't get completely clean in the dishwasher.

He wore his wiry blond hair pulled back in a ponytail, and a smudge clouded his thin-rimmed glasses.

"You and Kate. You're in love with her, right?"

He looked across the restaurant at Kate, carrying a tray of food from the kitchen. It made me angry that I was the one at fault, the one in love.

In November, Kate's parents had driven up from Florida for Thanksgiving. Before they arrived, Kate asked if she could tell her parents I was gay, to help them understand why she was having a hard time, why she seemed upset when they talked on the phone over the past few months.

"That's fine," I said, feeling my body tense as I said it. I hated that she was making me the problem.

I placed the knife and a clean fork onto a napkin, trying not to seem thrown by my co-worker's comment.

"No, I'm not in love with her."

I folded the napkin tightly so it wouldn't open when I placed it with the others in the basket. Before he could press any further, a customer flagged him down from a booth in his section. I watched Kate walking back toward the kitchen. I wonder now what was written across my face as I looked at her.

The one ritual I practiced the year Kate and I worked at the rib joint was drinking hot black tea.

One day after work, I noticed a strange smell in our apartment: something rotten, but an unusual rotten. A rotten I didn't recognize. Like a dead fish, but not quite.

In search of the smell, I walked around our small kitchen. I poked inside the garbage can; I opened the made-for-small-living-spaces refrigerator; I looked in cabinets. Finally giving up, I heated some water to make tea, planning to drink it in the bedroom where I could shut the door to keep out the mysterious rotting smell.

I didn't laugh when I opened the metal sugar tin I had inherited from my grandmother. I didn't laugh when I dipped a teaspoon into it. I didn't laugh when I found a small dead octopus buried in the sugar.

Holding my nose, I scooped it out. Its suction-cupped, purple-gray arms drooped over the sides of the spoon. The iron smell of its rotting tentacles had infused the entire half-pound of sugar.

"It's a joke," Kate said when I presented her with the octopus after she got home from her shift at the barbeque restaurant.

On Kate's trip to North Carolina to visit Brian the previous weekend, they'd tried a Japanese all-you-can-eat buffet for dinner, she told me as I held the octopus up in front of her.

To rib is "to joke," "to tease." At the time, I didn't think about how the joke meant she'd been thinking of me the whole time she'd been away: at dinner with Brian, when she first saw the octopus slick and gleaming on a bed of ice; on the car ride back to his apartment, the cold octopus wrapped in a napkin in her purse; falling asleep that night, as the octopus froze in a plastic bag in Brian's icebox; the next morning at breakfast, when she figured out the best way to transport the octopus back to South Carolina; and the 280 miles she drove with it—in a cooler in the passenger seat? in the trunk, as far away as possible? in a cup in the center console, its frozen body rattling against the sides of the plastic cup like a strangely shaped piece of ice?

It wasn't until my junior year in college that I learned there are two different creation stories in the Bible. In the first one, in Genesis chapter one, God took six days to make everything. In the second version, in Genesis chapter two, starting at verse four, it took only one day.

In the second story, God made Adam first, and then the rivers, every beast of the field, every bird in the air. In this version, Eve came last in the story, made of Adam's rib.

In the first story, though, God created Adam and Eve at the same time—and there was no mention of Eve being made of Adam's rib.

In my story, it wasn't long before Sarah realized she couldn't simultaneously love me and love God, and before Kate moved back to Florida and broke it off with Brian, who almost immediately married another girl. Years later—after I finished a master's degree in poetry, after Kate dated different guys, after I moved to LA, after Kate worked as a church youth minister, after I fell for other girls, after I moved to San Francisco, after she moved back to South Carolina, and after she started seminary—she called me one night to tell me something.

"I couldn't see myself clearly back then," she said.

I could feel her trying to find the right words, like a body bending over slowly to pick something up.

"I'm not straight," she said.

"What do you mean exactly?" I asked.

"I thought that since my experience was different from yours," she said, "—that I didn't have a feeling I might be gay when I was younger—it meant I must be straight."

Something opened inside me when she said it, like a jar—one with a seal so tight I was sure it couldn't be opened even when I knocked the top against the kitchen counter.

Hearing Kate name something in herself, what she'd resisted naming during the years we slept together and for years after, the hurt I'd felt, that I wasn't even fully aware I still felt, loosened.

Kate couldn't talk about her own queerness earlier in part because of the mainstream narrative of queerness beginning at birth. The queer creation myth *born this way* is often considered the *only* queer creation story.

"She can't help it," a mother says, in defense of her gay child.

"She was born this way."

This mother's defense has always bothered me because, while well-meaning, it implies a fault, a kind of birth defect in her daughter that the mother has learned to accept—*Poor girl, she can't help it that she's gay. If she could, she'd definitely be straight.*

Several years ago, I watched a YouTube video a friend posted on Facebook where two guys used the logic of Born This Way to convince people that gay people aren't actually terrible. In 2006, Chris Baker and Travis Nuckolls interviewed people on the streets of Colorado Springs, first asking if they think that gay people choose to be gay.

"I think it depends on what they grow up finding out," a young, white, baseball-cap-and-T-shirt-wearing guy with a goatee answers. "I think it's a choice later in life but it depends on upbringing."

Then Baker asks the guy, "When did you choose to be straight?"

"Umm," the guy responds, "that's a good call, man. I didn't choose to be."

In another interview, a blonde white woman wearing narrow sunglasses and silver hoop earrings says, "I don't know if people would *choose* to be gay."

It is this woman's answer that gets at one of the problems with the Born This Way/Choose to Be Gay debate: the idea that being gay is so terrible that you would never *choose* it.

This is not to say that Born This Way is not a creation story. It's a powerful and true story for many LGBTQ people. It's also a story that has convinced many people to accept LGBTQ people, an acceptance that has impacted the human rights movement in positive ways.

But, when Born This Way is the only story, the only queer creation myth, some LGBTQ people are excluded—to the point that they can't recognize their own sexuality, a part of their own identity.

Narratives of queerness are infinite. They do not always begin at birth. They cannot always be traced to childhood. A story can begin in medias res, as a wave begins in the middle of the ocean.

If an octopus's camouflage fails, if it's seen for what it really is, it resorts to ink, a thick black cloud, reimagining *protection*, what it means to live without ribs at the bottom of the sea.

When Kate told me she'd loved me, I felt our story bend, the way the ribs curve to encompass the lungs, the heart. In one story, we lived in a jar. In another story, we opened the lid and swam out into the darkness of the ocean.

VARIATIONS ON FALLING

You can't be sure if the girl fell for you at dinner or in the cemetery or a few days before when you lent her coins to buy a drink from the vending machine outside your classroom or when you both crawled out onto the roof, feet first, your shirt catching on the metal lip of the window frame, grazing your stomach.

If a girl falls for a girl, and no one notices her heart—the physical thing, not the metaphor—falling and picking itself back up in her chest (*lub-dub*, *lub-dub*).

If a girl grows up in a small town. No one hears of girls falling for girls there.

Your maternal grandmother, the woman you're named for, taught you how to differentiate between the sounds of certain things falling. "There, that's the rain coming in." And, "Did you hear my earring hit the ground?"

But she did not teach you how to recognize the sound of girls falling.

A girl herself may not notice (*lub-dub*, *lub-dub*) if the girl she falls for does not notice.

Or a girl wills herself not to notice.

You realize this is why you asked girls who did not often date girls to clarify things to you: "Am I as good in bed as the men you've slept with?"

After dinner with the girl you've only recently met. After you order pizza. After a group tour of the New Jewish Cemetery in Prague. After you hear she ended things with her boyfriend a few months back. After you see Kafka's grave. She tells you, taking a sip of her beer, how she'd slept with a girl once.

It is the summer before you move to California, before you leave the South. If you toss a coin up in the air, it is falling, though moving upward initially, from the moment it leaves your hand.

The two of you hurry across the city to a reading in an old theatre. You notice her cheeks holding heat. The bright redness of the theatre seats.

Later that night, she invites you up to her room to see the window access to the roof. You both crawl out into the dark. You talk near the ledge.

The Czech pronounce the sound of the heart beating *buch-buch*, *buch-buch*.

When you fall for a girl, you do not want anyone to see. You crawl out the girl's window onto the roof.

After the linden trees. After the girl's black cotton dress. Your sheer purple blouse.

"Maybe you should kiss me," the girl says on the roof (*buch-buch*, *buch-buch*). Ever since you crawled out her window you've been noticing the other windows to rooms where people may or may not be. You hear a song from someone's radio. When the vocalist oscillates slowly—you hear the low shift of pitch—is someone at the window watching?

If a girl falls for a fear—

Your grandmother told you several years before—the summer she was dying of throat cancer—that late one night from her bedroom window she saw your aunt kiss a woman on the beach. You remember this house your family rented years before for the weekend. You picture it through the glass window. Not your aunt kissing a woman, but the waves falling, breaking in the dark.

If fear is an inheritance. If certain types of falling are an inheritance, too.

After the girl's small, silver nose ring. Her painted fingernails. Her blue eyes. You ask her to come with you back inside. You hoist yourself up and crawl back through her window.

You never came out to your grandmother. "Something about it seems wrong," your grandmother told you, about a woman falling for another woman.

The girl, closing the latch to the window, says, "I think I read things wrong." You want to find the girl's mouth in an attempt to locate the word *wrong* at its source.

After seventeen bridges across the river. The braid in the girl's hair. Absinthe on fire in a glass.

The girl had a roommate and she could come back at any minute— after playing Scrabble in the yellow seventies-era lobby. Her roommate could have walked in and seen you finally kiss this girl, seen you on her orange-and-white-striped twin mattress, seen the girl take off your shirt. Seen the small pink scratch on your stomach where her window frame grazed you.

When bees swarm a linden tree, and no one's there to hear the sharp hum, do they make a sound? When you see *Láska* painted across a city wall, and you can't read Czech, does it still mean *love*?

Years later, you want to tell that girl you fell for why—after the two of you left Prague, after she insisted things between the two of you wouldn't work—you wanted to know her exact reasoning. You want to tell her that when the two of you crawled out onto that roof that first night you kissed, you could hear water breaking in the dark.

HOW TO IGNITE

My tongue is broken; / A thin flame runs under / my skin.

—Sappho

In seventh grade, I got a crush on the priest's daughter. I didn't call it a crush at the time. For a middle school girl in the South, or maybe anywhere in 1995, having a crush on another girl seemed impossible, a thing for which I didn't have a name.

Crush: the boy with blonde shoulder-length hair at the neighborhood pool. *Crush*: the cold orange soda my friends and I drank after school in the unfinished room above the garage, our tongues turning the orange of seventies shag carpet. *Crush*: the way my babysitter pressed the hot tip of her cigarette out, against the metal ashtray in her wood-paneled station wagon.

Elizabeth's family moved to town the summer before I started seventh grade, after my best friend's dad, the previous priest, received a call to another church in another state.

I grew up in the church, the way some people grow up in a neighborhood. Before my best friend moved away, we both lived in the older part of town within walking distance of seven churches. Unlike other kids at school who lived in subdivisions, with cul-de-sacs, tract housing, and gates at the entrances, my best friend and I walked through churchyards to find each other. We rode our bikes through graveyards, played basketball at the hoop behind the parish hall, started games of hide-and-seek in the Sunday school rooms. Every Wednesday afternoon we walked to choir practice. During certain liturgical seasons, like Lent, we ate supper at church, too.

We knew every hymn, every prayer, every place to hide. We knew every mystery, too, like "The Passion," the story of Jesus's last days on Earth and his suffering on the cross.

Passion, from the Old Occitan word *passio*: violent love.

That's the way it hit me when I first saw Elizabeth, in the green hallway, on my way to French class in the trailers behind the eighth-grade classrooms: *violent love*, as in distorting, the fluorescent lights humming above us in plastic panels, as in I didn't see anyone else against the long wall of green lockers, as in strong, an ocean wave, our school's mascot, the kids pushing their way through the halls, as in impatient, the teacher standing in the doorway, the hall bell about to ring above us.

Elizabeth was a year older than me, and in middle school a year seemed like a particularly long time. I thought that by eighth grade, girls had learned things about love that all seventh-grade girls didn't know yet. A few months into our friendship Elizabeth taught me how to break up with a boy. "If you don't like him, you should just tell him," she told me, as if what I wanted was as simple as saying the words.

"I'll show you," she said.

We sat cross-legged on her carpeted bedroom floor. She called my boyfriend, Paul, and pretended to be me. When he answered, she motioned for me to move closer to her, so I could hear.

"I don't want to go out anymore," she told Paul.

I could smell her hair—blonde and shoulder-length, parted down the middle. It smelled good, clean. I looked at her hands around the receiver, her nails short and bitten, something we shared, something we'd noticed about each other when we'd first met. Twirling the phone cord around her finger as she talked, Elizabeth made breaking up sound easy.

The first time I spent the night at Elizabeth's house we went to the grocery store with her mom before dinner. In the produce department Elizabeth picked up a pomegranate, a fruit I'd never seen before. In her hand, it looked like an apple. But, where a stem would be, a spiked opening appeared instead—a hardened flower without stamen or pistil.

"They're so good," she said. "You eat the seeds. I'll show you."

When we got back to her house, her mom cut off the unfamiliar fruit's spiked top on their kitchen counter, scored it into six sections, and pulled it apart, revealing what looked like hundreds of little red beads, enough to make a necklace.

"Try one," Elizabeth said, handing me a small red seed that she'd pulled from the pith to eat.

The seed was delicate, thin, and, when I put it in my mouth, easily broken. The knife her mom had used dripped pink.

Pomegranate, from the Latin *pomum* and *granatum*: seeded apple, fatal fruit, food of the dead, seed of the imprisoned, keeper of Persephone. In German, *granada*: an explosive shell used in warfare.

When "If You Wanna Be Happy" came on the radio in their kitchen that night, I thought Jimmy Soul's personal point of view was ridiculous. I thought I might be mishearing it, mistaking "never" for "you better," the way I misheard Gloria Estefan's "loved to hear the percussion" as "loved to hear her passion."

Elizabeth sang the refrains, and I laughed when she did the dialogue between Soul and one of his back-up singers near the end of the song.

On the 1963 album cover to Soul's hit single, the circles inside the *p*'s of "happy" form two eyes, and a line curves under the word to make a smile.

On one of the first really warm days of spring, I was an acolyte at an outdoor service. After processing up the grass aisle carrying the tall brass cross, I took my seat next to the priest, Elizabeth's dad. The bright grey headstones glimmered with sun. Elizabeth and several other eighth-graders sat in the front row in squeaky metal folding chairs. The azalea bushes bloomed bright pink, and all the girls wore sundresses.

I don't know what came over me. Maybe I overheated from wearing a long white robe over my dress. Maybe my serotonin levels shot up too quickly, my brain forgetting how to handle so much sun after months of grey winter days.

Or perhaps I went back in time, when *passion* was a verb, from the Old French *passionner* and the German *passien*: to torment, to torture, to want to the point of grief.

We might have been singing "Come Thou Fount of Every Blessing" or "Light the Fire" or "Purify My Heart." Whichever song the organist played on his portable keyboard set up in the grass made me feel suddenly ignitable. Oh Eros, oh thin flame, oh melter of our limbs. My body felt liquid, like there wasn't a single bone inside. Without thinking of the consequences, during the last hymn, I mouthed "I love you" to Elizabeth.

Still in my white acolyte robe, I walked straight up to Elizabeth after the service, trying to remember the way she'd broken up with Paul for me, on the phone months before.

"Did I trick you?" I asked her. And before she could answer, I said, "Olive juice."

I didn't wait for her to say the phrase back to me—for her to feel how she pushed her tongue off the back of her front teeth to say *olive*, to recognize how her mouth would open the same way if she said *I love*.

I didn't give her the chance to question me, to sound out *juice*, to feel the way her lips pursed as if she might take a drink, as if she'd said *you*.

I took the grenade of *I love you* carefully back, the shrapnel repacked tightly in its shell. Until I'd said it, I hadn't fully realized how dangerous those three words were for a girl to say to another girl.

The following Sunday after church I rode my pink ten-speed bike to a restaurant on the old town square to meet up with a group of eighth-grade girls, including Elizabeth, for lunch. We all ordered chicken fingers and fries, which the waitress brought to us in red plastic baskets. I was the only seventh-grader at the table, and I felt proud, like I knew the things they knew, even though I was a whole year younger.

After lunch we rode our bikes to Jane's house to find her parents' cigarettes. Our bike tires kicked up the gravel in her driveway, leaving lines in the dirt.

Some of the girls opened a window in the upstairs bathroom and smoked in the shower. I waited until we rode our bikes to Azalea Park, the same park where I'd first kissed a boy the year before. Standing on the grass in the circle of girls, I took a few puffs of the cigarette we passed around to share.

After leaving the park we rode to Holly's house, a few blocks away from church. I had about an hour before junior high youth group started. The eighth-grade girls were moving up to senior high youth group that week, so they didn't have to be at church until dinner.

Holly thought her mom wouldn't notice if we took a little pour of liquor from each bottle in their cabinet. That way all the bottles will look the same, she said. In a plastic cup, she poured a little vodka, a little gin, a little tequila, a little whiskey, a little pour of everything on the shelf. As we walked down the empty road from Holly's house to church, we passed the cup from girl to girl. It was like communion, the way all of us drank from the same cup. When the cup came to me, I could smell the way the alcohol would burn my throat. I put the cup to my lips, closed my eyes, and took a sip.

We reached the steps outside the church parish hall with ten minutes to spare, before I had to go inside. One of the girls asked the rest of us if we knew that you could use a cigarette lighter to burn a smiley face onto your skin, as if the smiles on our faces weren't enough.

"I'll do it," I said, surprising myself at how quickly I volunteered.

I can't remember if I asked Elizabeth to do it or if she volunteered. Regardless, the only way I was going to let someone burn me was if she was the one doing the burning. There was something comforting in knowing I'd share the hurt with her. Elizabeth and I had started taking guitar lessons together from a parishioner at church a few months earlier. I thought about the way the tips of our fingers hurt and sometimes bled after practicing. I thought about the way we compared the calluses on our fingertips, how, when we peeled off the hardened skin like the rind of a fruit, the skin underneath was pink and tender.

I sat down on one of the brick steps of the church and pushed up my shirtsleeve before I could change my mind. Elizabeth sat down beside me while the other girls circled around us. One of the girls pulled a lighter out of her jeans pocket and handed it to Elizabeth.

"Are you sure about this?" Elizabeth asked me.

"Yes."

Elizabeth pulled her thumb across the serrated spark wheel of the lighter several times until a flame flicked and stayed.

"Hold the lighter upside down until the top of it gets really hot," one of the girls instructed her.

"Are you okay?" Elizabeth asked me, insistent in her concern.

"I'm fine," I said, the liquor still warm on my breath.

Elizabeth moved her hand closer until she finally touched the hot metal top of the lighter to my upper arm, halfway between my elbow and my shoulder. Without thinking, I yelled and pulled away from her. The burn felt deep and permanent. But all that appeared on my skin seconds later was a faint pink curve. The lighter wasn't on my skin long enough to make the eyes or the full curve of the mouth. The mark looked indifferent, I thought, nothing like a smile.

"Do it again," I told Elizabeth, "I won't move this time."

The girls looked on in anticipation, the way people circle around a bonfire, a primordial fascination with things on fire.

Elizabeth ran her thumb across the little metal gears to get the lighter hot again. When she moved closer to me on the steps, I tried not to flinch.

I wanted desperately to forget the way the metal of the lighter had eaten at my skin minutes before. How my skin had seemed to melt, like wax, under the heat. As much as I tried not to think about it, though, I couldn't stop myself, and I pulled away from her a second time when she touched the lighter to my arm. Another faint curve appeared on my skin, an inch above the other one.

"This time, don't let me pull away," I told Elizabeth, determined to make it work.

"Are you sure?" she asked, looking at the two other burns.

"Yes," I said, with a surety I rarely had when answering questions.

This time, the third time, I wanted to get it right. She held my wrist with one hand and pushed the lighter into my upper arm with her other hand until I pulled away from her for good, sure that the metal had burned down to the muscle this time, singeing it black.

"There. It worked," I said, smiling when I looked down at the eyes and perfect mouth that had begun to pucker and pinken on my arm. The failed attempts looked delicate, already starting to blister—two necklaces to accentuate the bright face that smiled inches above them on my arm.

As I walked alone into the air-conditioned cool of the dimly-lit church parish hall for junior high youth group, leaving Elizabeth and the other eighth-grade girls behind me in the sun, I didn't know then how I would have to hide the burns from my parents, how the third burn—the worst burn—would get badly infected a few weeks later, how I would lie to my mom, insisting the burn was from a curling iron I used at a sleepover, how the eighth-grade girls would start high school so soon, how Elizabeth and I would grow apart, how a few years later the two smaller scars on my arm would completely disappear, how the worst burn wouldn't ever heal correctly, the scar still visible on my arm twenty-one years later.

A pool, a ripple. The scar from the burn catching light like water. *Burn*, a noun in Old English, meaning a stream or river. *Because I prayed / this word*: / I want, Sappho wrote, I asked a girl for a river, a burn to mark the fire I could not speak.

LIMBO

Limbo: the place DC Comics' forgotten heroes go when they haven't appeared in print in a long time. In the comic book *Animal Man* #25, released in July 1990, the superhero Gay Ghost waits among other forgotten heroes in Limbo. He's a ghost in a place full of ghosts.

For years Kate and I lived in limbo, from the Latin *limbus*: an edge, border, or margin. One night the moon cast a faint light on the thin white bed sheets, barely illuminating our bodies. The room was dark, like the darkness just beyond a campfire in the middle of the woods. Our hair, still wet from a bath, made our pillows damp and cool.

An hour earlier, when Kate said she was going to join me in the bath, I'd hesitated. My hesitance: a question of classification. At what point in a bath are two girls no longer straight? When one girl, washing her face, smears her mascara? When the other girl, with the tip of a damp washcloth, wipes it clean?

Feeling my reluctance, Kate pushed against it, got into the bath, and leaned her back against my legs, as if to say the space between us was thin, barely there.

Gay Ghost first appeared in the January 1942 issue of *Sensation Comics*. As popular culture historian Ron Goulart notes in the

Comic Book Encyclopedia, DC Comics most likely did not intend for the *gay* in Gay Ghost to suggest anything about the superhero's sexuality. Instead, the comic book publisher most likely meant for the word to signify this superhero's lighthearted, dashing demeanor, or maybe the ostentatious and colorful quality of his clothing.

Junior year, Kate's shirts started to fall off her shoulders, which were becoming more slender, delicate. Her cheekbones were becoming more pronounced, too, and she hardly slept. Some nights, she made her voice so quiet, so thin that I couldn't distinguish it from the wind outside. "Quieter," she told me, when I spoke. "They'll hear us."

Sometimes I forgot I had a body. Or all I could think about was that I had a body. Limbo, from the root word *limb,* any organ or part of the body.

Out of our fear of being heard or seen in bed together, Kate and I became more and more like ghosts.

In the 1979 best-selling memoir *Where Does a Mother Go to Resign?*, Barbara Johnson, a conservative Christian whose son came out as gay, writes, "Finding out about a gay child is agony, it's almost like having a death in the family. When someone dies, you can bury that person and move on with your life. With homosexuality, the pain seems never-ending." Both dead and undead, the child is disembodied, a ghost in his mother's story.

By 2004, Johnson's book had sold over 250,000 copies, and new readers continue to publish Amazon reviews, including this five-star review from February 14, 2017, titled "An 'All Moms Must Read'": "A beautiful thoughtful gift this book would be for Valentine's day for multiple persons who care or don't care about socially and political correctness anymore . . . Not when it comes to family! Love this book."

Gay Ghost's story begins like this: donning a bright blue bodysuit that shows off his muscular biceps and thighs, with yellow-capped sleeves and color-coordinated wrist cuffs, a tight red vest, a thick black belt, lavender boots and a matching cape, Keith Everett, an eighteenth-century Irish nobleman, set out on horseback to propose to the love of his life, Deborah Wallace. On the road to meet Deborah, though, Keith gets robbed and shot. Not far from there, Deborah, out on horseback with her father's men, hears the pistol shot and rides closer to investigate.

In the comic panel Deborah, blonde-haired and crying, kneels in the dirt road and holds Keith's hand as he's dying. The angle and tight frame of the next comic panel shows them both from the neck up, and so, for a moment I confuse Keith's red vest for a red dress, the neckline dipping to a fashionable V. For a second, I see two women about to have their last kiss.

When our friends were in the next room, only a wall's distance away, I slipped into the shower with Kate, as if passing through a wall. No one could see me. As steam filled the room, enveloping us in a warm fog, I slipped into Kate's body without anyone knowing.

When DC Comic's Keith Everett died, he became a ghost, completely white—no color filling in the black lines of him in the comic panel. No blue cloth holding tightly to his arms and legs. No lavender cape catching air as he rode his horse into the woods. As a ghost, Keith spoke with his ancestors, The Secret Council of the Dead, and begged their shadowy forms to allow him to return to earth to be with Deborah. The Council agreed, but Keith would have to wait.

When Kate first kissed me, I understood all of a sudden how separate I'd been from my body. I kissed her, and I wished I could trade places with every straight person in the world, that I could be proud to love her where everyone could see.

In 2004, queer theorist Lee Edelman published a book called *No Future: Queer Theory and the Death Drive.* Edelman argues against our culture's insistence on the child as the embodiment of innocence, the "possibility of a future." When I was with Kate, I didn't think about the future—partially because I couldn't imagine a future in which the two of us could be together. But also because I was so present that I wasn't thinking of the future. In the secrecy of her room, the only thing in the small-town darkness was us.

The title of a 2005 article on Focus on the Family's website reads: "When a Loved One Says, 'I'm Gay': The Stages of Grief." One mother describes the wind being knocked out of her, as if a part of her vanished like a ghost, when her child came out to her: "I felt as if I had been kicked in the stomach. All of my air went out of me. I wanted to die."

As a kind of epigraph (epitaph?), the article begins with an excerpt from Psalm 46, verses I've heard read at funerals: "God is our refuge and strength, a very present help in trouble. Therefore we will not fear though the earth gives way, though the mountains be moved into the heart of the sea, though its waters roar and foam, though the mountains tremble."

When Keith Everett finally gets to be with Deborah again, she's not the same girl, and he isn't the same either. Over eighty years have passed since Keith died in the road, and Deborah is dead and gone, but her last living descendant, her namesake, is alive and beautiful.

When Keith, as a ghost, approaches this younger Deborah Wallace, he calls out, *Darling!*, unaware that she isn't his Deborah—he doesn't realize that eighty years have passed since he died. The younger Deborah calls out to her fiancé, Charles Collins, for help. But in that same moment—how fortuitous!—German spies attack and kill Charles. Keith, leaning over Charles's dead body, quite like Deborah did over his body in that dirt road eighty years earlier, takes over Charles's body in order to save Deborah from the spies—before she even realizes Charles has been killed.

So, here's where Keith becomes Gay Ghost: he can now leave and re-enter Charles's body, materialize and dematerialize at will. He can finally be with Deborah Wallace again, albeit a different Deborah Wallace than he first fell in love with so many years before.

Even though Kate and I kept our secret for many years, we didn't always love each other during those years. We learned too late that the loss of each other was one of the consequences of living in limbo.

Revived characters, superheroes who return to print again, get to leave Limbo, the comic book purgatory. In that 1990 issue of *Animal Man* though, Gay Ghost says that he doesn't want to leave Limbo and come back to life. "*Gay* means something different now," he says. "I don't want to be Gay Ghost anymore, not if being gay means loving a man."

While far less legitimatized than conservative Christianity, The Spiritual Science Research Foundation claims that 85% of gay people are possessed by ghosts. They believe women are attracted to other women "due to the presence of male ghosts in them." The SSRF, like other conservative religious groups, says, "Homosexuality can be overcome by regular spiritual practice."

In 1990, at the same time Gay Ghost refused to come back to life, thousands of gay men were dying of AIDS. According to the CDC, by 1993 there were over 200,000 reported cases of AIDS in the US, and "as of December 31, 2000, 774,467 persons had been reported with AIDS in the United States; 448,060 of these had died." In 2012, Ryan Conrad, American artist, activist, and scholar, created an experimental AIDS documentary project: *Things Are Different Now*. Conrad superimposes portraits of his friends over archival video footage from the early nineties' ACT UP political funerals and protests. The superimposition creates an evanescent, haunting effect in the images, as if the men in the photographs are disembodied spirits. I remember this eerie effect happening accidently when I used a film camera growing up—before digital photography. Double exposure, the film processor told me, when I flipped through my strange, ghost-like photographs at the CVS counter. Marty Fink, a queer scholar who studies the early archivist histories of HIV/AIDS, writes, "[Conrad's project] addresses [the] yearning for ghosts by autobiographically lamenting the incomprehensibility of losing all one's friends to government neglect and homophobia."

David Levithan's 2013 young adult novel *Two Boys Kissing*, like Conrad's project, gives voice to gay ghosts. A Greek chorus of a generation of gay men who lost their lives to AIDS narrate the story of two seventeen-year-old boys attempting to set a new Guinness World Record for the longest kiss: "We were once the ones who were living, and then we were the ones who were dying. We sewed ourselves, a thread's width, into your history." The library shelving tag on the side of the book reads: *Child bk*. When I was a child, I never saw a book like this one on the shelf. In this way, stories themselves can be ghosts.

In college, when I first read that sexuality existed on a spectrum, for a second I misread *spectrum* as *specter*, an apparition. In our twenties Kate and I were so good at living in limbo, we couldn't imagine leaving. We slept in limbo. We talked in limbo. We made friends in limbo. When comic book characters are in Limbo, they don't realize that they're there. It wasn't until years later that Kate and I realized how we'd been like ghosts, how we had worked hard to make certain things in ourselves invisible. It wasn't until years later that we realized that part of the reason we were in limbo was because we lived in a culture where queer lives are erased. In Limbo, we had lived as wisps, faint traces of smoke on the horizon.

FIRE HOUSE

The summer my friend Allison broke her left arm and had to learn to do everything with her right hand, our parents signed us up for a week of Bible School. Allison and I were five years old, and it was as hot as a tin roof in July.

The first day the Bible School leaders split us up by age group, and our class spent most of the morning in an air-conditioned trailer behind the blue one-level church. The congregation didn't have the money to build on to the original wood structure, so they bought a few trailers to put in the grass lot behind the sanctuary for Sunday school classes and programs like summer Bible School.

Most of the week we must have sung Bible songs, colored Bible story coloring sheets, and played Bible story games in the trailers behind the church. Pin the tail on the donkey Jesus rode in to Jerusalem. Hot potato with a hymnal. Simon Says bow your head for prayer.

Alison learned to cut with right-handed scissors.

I don't remember the singing or the games, though. My only memory of the whole week was an older boy flicking on and off the lights in the trailer one morning.

He locked the door and yelled, "I'm going to set this trailer on fire!"

It wasn't the threat of fire that scared me exactly. It was the other kids' screams, the rough, tight-knit carpet under my knees, leaving impressions on my skin.

This was my first memory of panic.

In third grade, my town's local fire department parked an Inter-active Fire & Life Safety Trailer on the center of the field behind our elementary school. Similar to the D.A.R.E. presentations we'd heard in the school auditorium in fifth grade, the simulation trailer was part of an awareness and prevention program in public schools. The small white trailer was designed to resemble a house, equipped with a kitchen, a bed, a hallway, and several doors. We were meant to learn how to escape a burning house.

At first, the presentation seemed exciting, a chance to go out-side and miss the day's math lesson. Behind our teacher, Mrs. Danzler, my class filed out of the one-story brick school building and crossed the athletic field, making our way over to a group of firefighters in full uniform. I knew they were the good guys, the ones saving cats out of trees and putting out fires with long hoses, like the ones I'd read about in books, but, up close, they looked scary in their big helmets, boots, and sooty, full-body suits. One firefighter showed us the yellow and red hatchet they used to break down doors. "In a few minutes you'll crawl inside this door one by one on your hands and knees," he told us, his voice booming. "It's best to stay as low as you can," he said, as he got on his hands and knees to show us, "because heat rises real quick."

As I stood in line waiting for my turn to crawl through the small trailer, my palms started to sweat. My best friend got out of going through the simulation. She had bad asthma, and our teacher thought the "smoke" might set it off. More than the strange oxygen masks, the large men in overwhelming suits, or the images of flames on the side of the trailer, what scared me most was the thought of crawling through a small space that could close in on me, the thought that I might not be able to find my way out.

I don't remember much of the inside of the fire simulation

house—the stove, the pattern of the bedspread, the pictures on the walls—except for the tight-knit carpet under my knees, as I followed the classmate in front of me through the small door at the back of the smoke-filled trailer.

It was fake smoke, of course. The kind they use for magic shows, concerts, and plays. The Christmas before I had first seen and smelled fake smoke as I sat in the audience watching "The Nutcracker." Up from the smoke, a horrifyingly human-sized mouse king appeared on stage amidst a nail-biting music score. My short-lived ballet lessons that year had not prepared me for that.

Despite being "fake," the smoke smelled like it could do some damage. Crawling through the tiny simulation house, the smell of the smoke was overwhelming—like a new plastic toy or a freshly-opened can of tennis balls—but stronger, like I was *inside* the can of new tennis balls or sealed in a plastic bag with a plastic toy. The door we entered on one end of the trailer was small, less than half the size of a regular door. Ever since seeing *Willy Wonka & the Chocolate Factory*, I had a recurring dream that when I walked towards a door, it started getting smaller, until my head touched the ceiling and my knees pressed tightly against my chest. The whole corner of the room shrunk, and I worried that I'd never fit through the door and get out.

I had my first panic attack the summer after sixth grade, when I first kissed a girl.

I had my second panic attack my senior year in high school, when I told my boyfriend that I kissed a girl in middle school. I had my third panic attack my junior year of college, when I started sleeping with a girl.

Panic can feel like a kind of fire, burning you out from the inside.

My anxiety and depression surrounding the fear of my sexuality got so bad the year after college that my mom took me to her doctor, a family medicine doctor. I resisted her suggesting that I see a doctor, as I saw it as an indication that she thought I should take anti-depressants—I didn't need medicine, I insisted; I just needed to get a better job, move out of the studio apartment I shared with Kate, move to another city, another state—but my mom didn't take no for an answer.

My mom's doctor came in to the room, a light blue window-lit exam room where I'd been waiting for a few minutes, my feet hanging off the edge of the paper-covered exam chair.

"So, tell me what's going on," the doctor said. Despite the kindness in her voice, I felt reluctant to tell her things. I was only there to appease my mom.

"I've just been really stressed lately," I said, trying not to cry. "I work at a barbecue restaurant and it's just stressful some days." During that year, I was often trying not to cry. I forced down the tears beginning to well up inside me.

Swarming with anxiety, I ate sparingly—not to make myself thin, but thinness was a result nonetheless. I turned nauseous with anxiety.

I became so thin I could slip through the smallest of spaces. I slipped out of my clothes, I slipped in and out of rooms without anyone noticing.

The air inside buildings felt thin. My breathing and heartbeat quickened. Suddenly, I forgot how to walk through a room, sit at a table, sleep in a bed. At night, shaking with panic, I tried to teach myself how to breathe, how to slow down the beating of my heart.

In college, sitting on the edge of Kate's bed one night, she tried to talk me down from a panic attack. "Just start talking," she said.

I shook my head, started to curl up in the fetal position. She held me, didn't allow me to lie down, and said, "It's okay."

"It's not . . ." My voice trembled and my teeth chattered. I didn't think I could get out a whole sentence. "I can't," I told her.

"What's the worst thing that's going to happen?" she said.

"I just . . . I feel like . . . I feel like I'm . . . my heart is beating too fast." My words were interrupted with the fear that my teeth, in their sharp chatter, would clamp down on my tongue or the inside of my cheek.

Kate stayed beside me, and slowly, I was able to get out more words, something I'd never been able to do before during a panic attack. Usually, I just lay in bed and shook until I fell asleep, and when I woke up in the morning, I was okay—until it happened again.

Sitting next to Kate on the edge of her bed, the more I was able to talk, the less my body shook until, suddenly, I realized I wasn't shaking at all.

Imagine an Interactive Panic Safety Trailer outside of every elementary school in every state. Inside, every kid who might at some point become so afraid of their sexuality that they tremble like a flame. Here, we will learn how to get through panic, that house on fire. We will learn how to get through our own bodies. We'll practice crawling through panic, so we'll know we can make it out the other side. We'll practice breathing into a paper bag, watching it expand and contract like the lungs inside our chests. We'll hold a lit candle in our hands and learn how to see panic as an object, not an abstraction in our head. We'll practice saying what we're afraid of out loud, to name the panic for what it is. We'll learn about medications we can take if the panic gets too big, like a house engulfed in flames.

When a man leans out his car window and aims a slur at us like a loaded pistol. When we're holding hands on the sidewalk in our city and a kid spits on us as he walks by. When someone threatens to set us on fire. When a man holds up a sign on a street corner that says, *Fags All Burn in Hell.* When our families don't know how to love us. When our friends don't know how to respond to us. When our lovers can't love us because they're afraid. They're so afraid that they don't recognize their fear as fear. Their fear is so deep inside of them that they don't know to name it. The fear is so hot that they pull away from it, instinctively, like a hand on a hot stove. Somewhere along the way, they have been taught to pull away like this.

Some days, we feel our panic go from a fire in a house to a house on fire.

But, with practice, when our breath begins to thin, we can focus on the thinness. We train ourselves to focus on the thinness. We focus on our breath until we can hold it in our hands.

Imagine an infinite line of luminaries lining the streets of every city and every small town at night. Imagine we are the candles. Imagine we are the hands. Our breath is so thin it can fit inside a small bag. Each bag is like a lung. How reliable our lungs are most of the time, we think; we don't even notice them inside our chests.

When we look up from our breathing, we suddenly notice something we haven't seen before—the endless line of luminaries in either direction, on both sides of the street. For as far as we can see, every street is on fire with panic, a panic we recognize. Our breathing slows, but we don't notice it slowing. We are trying to count the number of lights. Not just our individual panic, but other people's panic, too. Our heartbeats begin to slow, too, as our hearts, our valves, our vessels, our blood remember their regular rhythms, their ordinary pumping. We speak to the person next to us, and the person next to them. "Look at how far the light goes," one person says, pointing in the distance.

I'm not saying that we're not scared, that the fear is completely gone, that it won't resurface, but we can see that we aren't alone in it.

VARIATIONS ON PRAISE

When I didn't name my desire, *praise* became a complicated act: Do I tell the girl I love how much I like her hair pulled back in a messy bun? Do I hold on to the time she told me how pretty I looked in that particularly red shirt? Do I keep her praise like a flower drying upside-down and pinned to the corkboard over my dorm room desk?

In high school, I sang in the praise band at our church. I sang praise songs to God in front of hundreds of people. I'd joined the church choir when I was eight or nine years old. Some people raised their hands and some closed their eyes, but I just sang.

In elementary school one of my best friends played "As the Deer" on the grand piano in her living room. Afternoon after afternoon. That year, she had a crush on a boy named Tony. She told me that as she played the praise song for hours—her fingers memorizing every key—she thought about Tony, how she longed to worship him.

In the South, a praise house is a small meetinghouse where people participate in nighttime services mainly devoted to song.

When I'm driving in the car and I scan through the stations on the radio, I sometimes hear a love song and misinterpret the context of the words. For a few lines, I cannot tell that it's a Christian praise song. At first I think someone is singing about their love for a person, not their love for God.

Kate, the girl I used to love, tells me years after we stop sleeping together that I never told her how nice her hands are. A boy she's recently started dating tells her how he loves her hands. I look at her hands, hold one of them in mine, and, say, "Yes, they are particularly nice hands." I wonder what else I didn't tell her when we were together, how—assuming I didn't have to say it for her to know—I failed to let her know how beautiful she is.

Is praise always an act of worship? A practice of adoration? A performance? When you love someone in secret, do you fail to love them?

In a photograph of me from my twentieth birthday, I'm looking right into the camera and smiling. The candles on the birthday cake in front of me must have just been lit. I remember that Kate was taking the picture. I'm looking at the camera with so much devotion.

Praise is linked etymologically to *price*. I considered the price of loving Kate where everyone could see us: the potential losses, the judgment, the hurt. And so, I loved her in secret, a silence neither of us realized would come at so high a price.

THE ORGAN

so many members, so many parts, so many joints, so many sound conduits,
so much tonal effect, so many combinations, so many pipes, and all at one
touch
—*The Art of Organ Building, Tertullian (150–230 AD)*

In 1933 in Langenau, Bavaria, a church put a strange advertisement in the local newspaper: "Very price-worthy is the still wonderfully functioning church organ, which, if it cannot be sold for musical purposes, will make an excellent beehive."

Imagine a choir of bees inside an organ, producing pressure, so much wind from the whir of their wings that the keys and the pedals of the organ start to move.

Every Wednesday afternoon of my childhood I walked with my three best friends to choir practice at the 150-year-old Episcopal Church less than a mile from my house. In those sun-white afternoons, the church organist played hymns for us to practice. With our backs to the large paned second floor windows of the church hall, which overlooked the grassy graveyard below, my best friends and I matched each other's pitches.

In the weekly podcast *Secrets of Organ Playing*, host Dr. Vidas Pinkevičius, organist and composer, frequently starts each episode's discussion by asking his guests, "Do you remember how you first fell in love with the organ?" Peter Holder, Organ Scholar at

Westminster Abbey and organist at St. Paul's Cathedral in London, responds to this question in a recent episode by describing when he joined a local church choir as a child.

I, too, first fell in love with the organ when I joined the church choir at age eight. Every Sunday morning after kneeling at the altar for communion, I, following the line of people going back to their pews, walked behind the organ where the organist played a hymn. I watched the organist's hands sweep over the keys and pull the stops, while his feet glided across the organ's wooden pedals, as if he were dancing and playing several instruments simultaneously. It was mesmerizing to watch.

In middle school our church hired a new organist. With a master's and doctorate degree in music, he had studied the organ for years, composed his own music, and conducted orchestras all over the United States and the world: a study in Vienna, a concert and lecture series at the New York City Metropolitan Museum of Art, internationally-broadcasted choral concerts for the CBC.

After he was hired, people started coming to church early just to hear him play the prelude before the service started. People would stay after the processional, too, to hear him play. Many Sundays the congregation clapped after he hit the final notes with an exuberance I wasn't used to hearing at church. Tan and fine-featured, with short, dirty-blonde hair, our new organist exuded a kind confidence as he sat up tall in his black and white robe at the wooden organ. I thought he was beautiful. Movie star beautiful—like a young, tanner Greg Kinnear. The kind of beautiful that I wasn't used to seeing in my small Southern town. He was one of the first men I ever saw with volume in his hair.

In eighth grade, Elizabeth, the priest's daughter, the girl I had a crush on, passed me a note after our Wednesday afternoon choir practice. She'd written the note on pink construction paper and folded it in a way that middle schoolers spent hours perfecting: epistolary origami with one corner of the folded note tucked in to another fold to seal it. The thickness of the construction paper must have made it difficult to fold with precision, I thought, as I held the note in my hand. On the outside of the note, Elizabeth had written my first name with a horizontal *s* curved under it, another detail that made me think she'd taken her time in composing this note to me.

In the Museo Correr in Venice, there's a 1494 preserved positive organ with three stops and pipes made of paper. I imagine the sound of paper organ pipes vibrating. I imagine how paper carries sound.

I'd hung up the phone on Elizabeth a few nights before and I hadn't talked to her since. My birthday was coming up and because I was turning fifteen, my mom said I could invite four friends to a fancy dinner at a restaurant. Fifteen meant that I was getting my driver's permit, having my ears pierced, and getting my first car. So I'd called Elizabeth, the girl I had a crush on—she didn't know I had a crush on her, or if she suspected it, I never confirmed it. We were friends. But, when I invited her to my birthday dinner, she said she had other plans that night—she'd told another friend that she'd go over to her house to hang out. I was so hurt that she didn't consider cancelling her other plans—something I would have done without a second thought if she'd invited me to her birthday dinner—that, without thinking, I hung up on her, leaving the dial tone pulsing in her ear.

When Elizabeth handed me the pink note as we all hurriedly left the carpeted choir room in a rush down the narrow stairwell to the first floor, she laughed with her friend Corey. Elizabeth had barely looked me in the eye. It was how I'd passed notes to my friends a hundred times before: quickly, covertly, between classes, but because I'd hung up on Elizabeth a few nights before, I worried her laugh with Corey signaled something else, that they were laughing at me. I couldn't wait to get outside, walk home with my other friends, and open the note in my bedroom when I was all alone.

Inside, Elizabeth had written my name in purple letters at the top of the page and dotted the top and bottom of each letter with a red marker. My name looked happy up there on the top of the page. Inside the *a* at the end of my name, she'd drawn a smiley face. The note was long—taking up the whole page and the top of the back. "Hey sweetie! How's it going? Just great this way!" it began.

I breathed a sigh of relief as I sat on the edge of my quilted twin bed in my little attic room. But then, as quickly as I'd felt at ease, thinking Elizabeth wasn't mad at me for hanging up on her the other night, that she might have even cancelled her plans with her other friend and changed her RSVP to *yes* to my birthday dinner, the tone of the note shifted: "Why'd you hang up on me the other day? That was wrong! . . . You had no right to be mad at me! . . . I feel like you're mad at me b/c we're not as close as last year—well it's not my fault!"

In 1933 in Barnesville, Georgia, certain pipes in a church organ would not stop playing. An expert organ repairman travelled all the way from Boston to find out what was happening. As the *New York Times* notes, "It was discovered that moths had eaten the felt from the stops," the components that control the amount of pressurized air entering the organ's pipes. The sound from the pipes kept coming and coming.

After reading the note, I read it again. And, hours later, I couldn't get Elizabeth's words out of my head:

> *b/c I don't write you back all the time or*
> *b/c I don't call you all the time, b/c*
> *we never do anything, or we don't talk anymore!*
> *It's just getting old!*
> **_Chill Out_**_!!!_

It felt as though all the stops in my mind had opened, and I'd lost the control to close them. I couldn't stop thinking that Elizabeth had figured something out about me that I hadn't even named about myself and that she hated me for it.

An 1899 *New York Times* article describes "an altogether unaccountable tendency on the part of domestic cats to get into [church] organs, to remain in them regardless of hunger and thirst, to so dispose their bodies as to render futile the combined efforts of organ blower or organists to evoke music from the instrument, appears to have developed in widely separated sections of the country."

After reading the note from Elizabeth I wanted to crawl inside a space so small that no one could find me, and regardless of hunger or thirst, I wouldn't come out. I wanted to hide so that I never had to see her again.

Her nearly exclusive use of exclamation marks, her repetition of "because," her use of underlining and bolded print all seemed to make clear that she saw right through me. She knew I had a crush on her and she was tired of it. No, she was more than tired of it; she hated me for it. I panicked, fearing she'd figured me out, that she'd guessed my secret.

In 1905 in Middletown, New York, when the church organist played the first four bars of the opening hymn, mice came flooding out of the organ pipes, ran fearfully down the pulpit steps and down the aisles, and out the front doors the ushers opened into the street.

After I read the note from Elizabeth, fear flooded me until I thought it might literally pour out of me. Out of my bedroom, out of the house, down our dirt driveway, into the pine-lined streets, onto my neighbors' porches, into the ponds murky with algae and heat, into every church of every denomination in my small town.

I think of the organ and organ music as synonymous with church—but that wasn't always the case. In his history of the instrument, George Ashdown Audsley notes that the organ was first used in churches in the middle of the fifth century, possibly a little earlier. But not everyone wanted the organ, or other musical instruments, to be used in churches, just as some churches forbade dancing.

In 1906, the *New York Times* notes that one Puritan objected to the introduction of the church organ because it meant "worship by machinery." In the July 6, 1908 *New York Times* article "Annoy Pastor in Church," Reverend Dr. James Y. Boice, a minister at a Reformed Presbyterian Church in Philadelphia, argues that instrumental music, including the organ, has no place in the church. "In defiance of [the preacher's] wishes," though, as the *Times* reports, "when Dr. Boice walked up to the platform," the organist took his seat at the organ. When Dr. Boice led the congregation in singing the twenty-fifth Psalm, "the organ accompanied the singers." The organist's defiance continued throughout the service: "Following the reading of the Scripture, Dr. Boice called for the offering. Seeing that [the organist] was getting ready to play, he crossed to him, saying, 'Do not play the organ; there is not necessity for it.' And [the organist,] without replying, calmly looked the minister in the eye and began playing."

I'd thought hanging up on Elizabeth was an act of defiance, but when she wrote me that note, I realized I wasn't brave enough yet to say what I really wanted to say. When I wrote her back, it was just an apology.

Organists are part of a tradition of resistance. In 2013 Nick Johns, an openly-gay organist at Saint Brigid Catholic Church in Alpharetta, Georgia was given the option to resign or be fired after posting pictures of him and his fiancé and supporting marriage equality online. As noted by the *Georgia Voice*, "[Johns] was under suspension due to his Facebook profile being in public moral dissension with the teachings of the [Catholic] church."

In 2014 Colin Collette, who "began playing the organ at a Catholic church when he was twelve years old," lost his job as music director at Holy Family Catholic Community in Inverness, Illinois after announcing on Facebook his wedding to his long-time partner. Collette had been working at the church for seventeen years.

In 2016 Michael Templeton, organist and director of music ministry at St. Mary's Roman Catholic Church in Providence, Rhode Island was fired after marrying his partner. During the Sunday morning service after Templeton's dismissal, when the priest was in the middle of a prayer, a parishioner started singing the hymn "All Are Welcome." Other members of the congregation joined in, saying afterwards that this was "their way of speaking out against the firing."

Both the object of the organ and the queer person, objectified by the church, represent a pleasure that the church has equated with sin. Too much sound. Too much song.

While the organist at my childhood church didn't get fired because of his sexuality, several parents removed their children from choir when they found out that he was gay. One family pulled their three daughters out of choir, making it clear that they disapproved of the church's choice to let him stay. The organist eventually left our church and moved to a different church in a bigger city. When he left, our church hired another organist, a man with three children, a man married to a woman.

I imagine the kind of fear it takes to want someone gone, to remove your children from someone's presence. I thought about Elizabeth's note, how she wanted me gone. It's the kind of fear you can feel on the back of your neck, that you can hear in complete silence when you pass someone on the street. The kind of fear that vibrates like bees swarming the wind chest of an organ, building so much pressure inside that the pistons release, the pedals engage, the stops no longer able to stop that swell box from singing.

SPECTRUM

The impulse sprinklers had begun their evening rotations. Kate and I heard the sprinklers—like dogs vigorously scratching themselves—when we turned into Brian's parents' neighborhood. It was the only evidence that people lived in the nice but indistinguishable houses we passed.

Kate was in town for two reasons: to visit me and to take care of Brian's dog. Pets weren't allowed in the apartment complex where Brian lived, so his parents were keeping his dog for the time being—but this week they were on vacation. I'd started the second year of my master's at a university in South Carolina, Kate was waiting tables and living in Florida at her parents' house, and Brian was in his second year of graduate school in North Carolina.

In Brian's parents' kitchen I noticed commemorative state thimbles and spoons, thumb-sized cats, and dolls the size of teeth in a sectioned antique wooden box on the wall. Giving me a tour of the house, Kate and I went upstairs. I looked at the framed pictures of Brian and his sister on the walls. He had blond hair when he was little, which surprised me, since I only knew his dark hair and bearded face at twenty-four.

"I'm going to take a bath," Kate said.

Before I could question her, Kate shimmied out of her jeans, pulled her shirt over her head, unhooked her black lacey bra.

"Join me?" she said, tossing her matching black underwear on the floor beside the tub.

I stood in the doorway. Her skin was the white of interiority, the inside of things. I was all in my head. She looked beautiful, I thought, in a way that, even after knowing someone for years, can hit you unexpectedly. Kate and Brian's relationship was close to disintegrating—like a cotton nightgown translucently thin before it rips—but they were still together, and standing there in the doorway to the bathroom, I suddenly realized how much I didn't belong in Brian's parents' house.

Brian's parents' tub looked particularly nice: a white Jacuzzi bath with jets. But I hesitated when Kate asked me to join her. I imagined Brian's parents forgot something they needed for their trip—their swimsuits, a certain pair of shoes for a fancy dinner out. Brian's dog didn't bark when Brian's mom opened the front door. Her shoes didn't make any noise as she walked across the carpeted living room floor to the base of the stairs.

When Brian's mom stood at the bottom of the stairs—"Kate, is that you?"—Brian's dog finally barked.

"Hi! Yes, it's me," Kate called back, trying to sound calm.

We nearly fell over as we hurried to put on our clothes. As Kate walked downstairs, I waited upstairs, hoping I could go unseen. I estimated whether there was enough space for me to slide under the guest room bed. Every piece of clothing I was wearing stuck to my skin. Under my shirt, I felt a bead of water roll down my back. The bathtub was still full of water—in our rush to get dressed we had forgotten to drain it—and the floor was soaking wet.

But Brian's parents didn't forget anything. They didn't come home early. I didn't have to make myself disappear.

Kate's blonde hair was pulled back in a bun. A few tendrils had come loose and fallen at her neck. She leaned back in the tub and looked over at me, still standing in the doorway. Her cheeks flushed from the warmth. The mirror had fogged over, the walls were slightly wet, and I started to feel the heat from across the room.

"Are you sure you don't want to come in," Kate asked, pushing a ribbon of hair out of her face.

I knew I shouldn't be inhabiting this space with Kate, but I walked towards her. I imagined slipping off my shoes, my shirt, my shorts. Nearly losing my nerve, I stood there for a moment in my underwear. Kate watched me. My pulse was racing, like a current running through water.

Spectrum, from the Latin verb *specĕre*: to look, see. After loving in secret for so long, my sense of sight became heightened. I wondered—I looked at people and wondered—what people saw when they looked at me and what people were blind to, unable to recognize. When Kate, the person I thought saw me most clearly, looked at me junior year after we'd been sleeping together for months, and told me she was straight, I wondered if I were seeing things clearly. And now, years later, when Kate and I started sleeping together again, and Kate insisted she was still straight, I worried I was losing my ability to perceive reality.

I didn't get in the bath with Kate at Brian's parents' house. I didn't take off my clothes. For a moment, I didn't move out of the doorway. I stood on the threshold.

While Kate was in the bath, I looked at the photographs on Brian's parents' living room walls: a beach vacation, a high school graduation, a birth. I didn't want to think what Kate and Brian's kids would look like, but looking at pictures of him as a kid, I found myself imagining them: blond, green-eyed, tan.

That's when I heard it. A radio? A television?

I walked into the kitchen and flicked on the overhead light. Brian's dog followed behind me, his nails clicking on the floor. I walked around the room, trying to locate the sound, to make out the word I thought I heard. As I got close to the wall closest to the stairwell, I heard the voice again.

The voice was faint—maybe I'd misheard it; maybe it wasn't a voice at all. But then I heard it a third time and there was no mistaking it: *help*.

It sounded like a girl, a girl at least fifteen. I slowly pulled back the window curtain—just an inch—to look at the neighbor's house about fifteen feet away. Could they have been having a fight?

When I thought I saw *specter* the first time I read "sexuality exists on a spectrum," my misreading was not exactly wrong. Without realizing it, I'd seen something inherent in the word *spectrum*, something under the surface. In the Oxford English Dictionary, the etymology entry for *spectrum* reads: "see SPECTRE," and the first definition of *spectrum* is "an apparition or phantom; a spectre." Thinking about this etymological connection between *spectrum* and *specter*, I thought about what it might mean for the sexuality spectrum to be spectral in nature. Is it that a spectrum is a supernatural view of sexuality, one that's in opposition to "natural" laws, laws that operate with strict binaries: right or wrong, male or female, guilty or innocent? Or does the connection to the spectral imply the act of imagination, the ability to conceive of categories that at one time did not exist by name? Does it imply that one must suspend one's belief in clear distinctions, admitting that there are more than two possibilities for defining your sexuality?

When I stepped outside Brian's parents' house, it was dark and all the sprinklers were off. Afraid someone might be at the neighbor's window, or worse, in the bushes, I crept along the side of the house. I paused and listened for a minute, trying to find the voice, but the whole neighborhood was quiet, almost eerie. I hurried back inside, hoping that I'd just imagined the girl's voice in my head—at that moment, going crazy seemed like a better option than being right. But as I rounded the corner back into the kitchen, I heard the voice again.

I ran, my feet nearly slipping on the carpeted stairs. Upstairs, I found Kate still in the bath.

"Get dressed. There's a noise downstairs and it's freaking me out."

"What? What kind of noise?" Kate cupped her hands together and washed soap off of her face with a splash of water.

"A girl. A girl saying, 'help.'"

Kate laughed, "What?"

I realized how ridiculous I sounded, but I didn't want to be in the house any longer. I needed to get out.

"Come on. I'm serious!"

"Okay, okay, I'm getting out."

Ghost stories get at the difficulty people have with ambiguity. We want clear answers. We want proof. We want to draw a clear line between what is real and what must have been all in our heads. I have never been good at numbers, at being precise, so in conversations with close friends, I say what feels most true: my sexuality exists somewhere between *bisexual* and *lesbian/gay* on the spectrum, closer to *lesbian/gay*. But sometimes my lack of precision confuses people—*you realized your attraction to men wasn't real after you starting dating women, right?*

A close friend, a friend who identifies as liberal, endlessly open, told me that she doesn't believe in bisexuality. *If someone says they're bisexual, they're either lying or afraid to tell the truth.* For her, the stronger desire—for either men or women—is the identity.

When we walked into the kitchen, Kate, now dressed, immediately heard it, too: "Help."

"What could it be? Maybe it's—"

She pushed open the curtain on the window facing the neighbor's house.

"I already checked outside. There's no one there," I said, quickly closing the curtain.

"It sounds like it's coming from the garage."

I had seen the door on the inside wall of the kitchen when I'd tried to locate the sound earlier, but I hadn't known where it led— I'd guessed a closet.

We considered opening the door to the garage—maybe Brian's parents had left a radio on in there? Kate and I hovered beside the door. I worried what—or worse, *who*—we'd find if we turned the knob.

"I think we should leave. Seriously, let's go," I said.

I didn't give Kate much of an opportunity to object. Brian's dog lay on his dog bed, unaffected by the noise and our anxiety.

"I've got the keys to the car," I said, holding them up and walking towards the front door. "I'm leaving."

If there's no record of a relationship, did it ever really exist? For a long time, only Kate and I knew we had been together—and for years, Kate said she wouldn't name it that way, being together.

It wasn't until weeks later that, retelling what happened that night, I named the story a ghost story. When Kate told Brian's parents about the noise in their house, they paused strangely.

"What?" Kate asked, picking up on their hesitance.

"It's probably just superstitious," Brian's mom said, "but we bought an antique baby carriage at that run-down antique mall by the interstate—like the day before we left for our trip—and it's in the garage."

"It's freaky, right?" Kate said, as she relayed the story to me.

When I thought about it, the antique baby carriage, the strange voice, I thought about the difference between the words "carriage" and "stroller." How "carriage" held more darkness, more strangeness, how somehow it carried more possibility for loss. When I thought about the carriage, I thought about the girl, the voice the girl held inside her until she couldn't hold it there any longer. Was she holding onto the carriage or was it holding onto her? I imagined her eyes as sounds—like impulse sprinklers turning themselves on every night.

"I mean, there's got to be an explanation for it—one that's based in reality," I said, lying next to Kate in bed.

She moved closer for me to spoon her, pulled my arm around her waist, held my hand. Our nightshirts were specter-thin.

VARIATIONS ON MOOR

When school let out at the end of sophomore year, Kate and I drove to the beach. We knew we were close when we could smell the marsh. *Marsh*, from the Old High German *muor*, meaning both *swamp* and *sea*. A word that defies clear classification. A threshold landscape, an in-between, a place where water collects.

At sailing camp when I was twelve years old, at the edge of the marsh I learned to moor, to secure an Optimist to a dock, to tie sailors' knots: square knot, half hitch, becket bend.

The year we worked at the rib joint, when we lived only thirty minutes from the ocean, Kate and I never went to the beach, not once. That year, I worried Kate and I would never be together again, and, at the same time, I worried Kate would always be my mooring post.

Moor: both a rope and the act of tying a rope to fasten two things together.

At twelve, the Optimist I learned to sail looked more like a bathtub than a boat. When it was my friend's turn to steer, I sat in the hull, as I did in the bath. In a bathtub, though, I controlled the water, how deep I went, if my hair got went, if my whole body went under.

Every time we capsized, the boat tried to take us down with it. I swam to the surface, but the sail trapped me. In a panic, I kicked and paddled out from under it.

Like the name of the boat I sailed at camp, "optimist" was a word I used to describe Kate the first few years of our friendship. Being around her made me feel better. On the drive to the beach on the first day of summer after our sophomore year, Kate turned up the radio so loud I thought the speakers might break. We sang one song so recklessly there was no room for fear. Happiness swallowed me whole.

"There are many ways of being held prisoner," Anne Carson writes, "I am thinking as I stride over the moor."

Moor, from the root word *marr*, meaning *sea*. In the sea's connection to the root word *mer*, to die, I wondered if it was the ocean's ability to swallow me whole if it wanted to that made me decide to stop going to sailing camp.

Fear is a kind of ocean, a boundless expanse. Treading it like water, Kate and I had grown thin, weak.

"Pretend you are resting on top of the sea," my grandmother told me, as she showed me how to float in the ocean, my back flat and my arms outstretched. "I've got you," she said. "You're not going to float away."

A moor, like a marsh or swamp, is often considered wasted ground, an uncultivated area. Our door room senior year and then the studio apartment where Kate and I lived the year after, often felt this way—wasted, marred.

Literary scholar Hannah Godwin writes about the complicated associations with the swamp in the South. Historically viewed as a "morally dubious" landscape, a dangerous place for women in the South, a place which threatened the link between white Southern femininity and innocence, the swamp was also a site of refuge for outcasts in the South. In analyzing Eudora Welty's *Delta Wedding*, Godwin studies this ambiguity and sees the "wetlands as ripe for transformative encounters and moments of feminine revelation."

I wondered what Kate and I could have done differently. If, during those years we had driven the swampy back roads, seen the cattail beds at low tide, the heron, breathed in the smell of the marsh, that liminal space between the swamp and the sea. If we had made it to the ocean, watched it swell, felt it let go. If we had floated on top of it. If we had not been afraid.

Mooring, so close to *mourning,* to worry, to care, to utter a song of grief.

"People can't, unhappily, invent their mooring posts, their lovers and their friends," James Baldwin writes, "anymore than they can invent their parents."

One moors a vessel so as not to lose it to the sea. In this way, mooring allows us to keep things indefinitely.

When Kate and I drove to the beach on that first day of summer after our sophomore year, we rolled down our windows when we were close. The day brimmed with so much optimism I could hear it. In the marsh, the needlerush and cordgrass sang, like knives being sharpened by the wind.

BLOOD MONEY

All gods who receive homage are cruel. All gods dispense suffering without reason. Otherwise they would not be worshipped. Through indiscriminate suffering men know fear and fear is the most divine emotion. It is the stones for altars and the beginning of wisdom. Half gods are worshipped in wine and flowers. Real gods require blood.
                    —Zora Neale Hurston, *Their Eyes Were Watching God*

The clinician instructed me to squeeze a green foam ball to make the cephalic vein more visible in my right arm.

"That's good," she said, feeling my blood start to come to the surface of my skin under her blue-gloved fingertips.

To avoid seeing the butterfly needle—closer to the thickness of a toothpick than the pin-prick needles I knew from routine doctor's visits as a child—puncture my skin and enter my vein, I looked around the tiled-floor room at the rows of other people, their legs elevated in blue pleather reclining chairs like the one I was sitting in.

To hold the needle in place, the clinician taped the venipuncture tube onto the inside of my forearm—a place where the skin is thinner and more tender than other places on the body, and so I already dreaded the quick rip of the tape when this was all through. The clinician clipped the tubing to momentarily stop the blood flow while she attached more tubing to the plasma extraction machine. When all the tubing was in place, she turned on the plasmapheresis machine.

I watched the long extension of plastic tubing turn dark red as my blood left my arm and coursed up to the machine. The pump on top of the machine spun quickly, pulling my blood through the tubing and into the centrifuge. I started to feel slightly dizzy and so I tried to focus on the coldness of the room, the perpendicular lines of the floor tiles. I tried to find Kate, who was a few rows over, just out of sight. I imagined both of our blood spinning dizzily inside the centrifuges until our platelets and plasma separated from our red blood cells.

Kate had found the plasma center online—she'd seen a billboard for it: "New Donors . . . Make $100 This Week!"—and even though it seemed like a questionable option, we needed the money. We were waiting tables at the rib joint, but some shifts the tips barely covered the cost of gas for the drive from our apartment to the restaurant. During a lunch shift the week before, I overheard a customer telling his friends at a booth in my section that waitresses make an hourly rate so they didn't need to leave a tip on their forty-dollar tab.

"They don't even work that hard," he told them.

After they paid, I gave them their change, and they walked out of the restaurant. When I went to clean their table, I found a single quarter on top of their printed receipt, which felt more insulting than no tip at all.

I wanted to run out the door of the restaurant after them, the smell of rib smoke following me into the parking lot. I'd wave my arms as they got into their car, "Wait! Wait!"

The guy in the passenger side seat—the guy who'd told his friends not to tip—would roll down his window. He'd sit up a little in his seat, lean to the side, pat the back pocket of his jeans, suddenly worried he might have forgotten his wallet or cell phone in the restaurant.

When I got to the car window—my black work shirt hiding the barbeque stains from a long shift—I'd put out my closed hand, holding what he left, and when he put out his hand, palm up, thankful and a little curious as to what he'd forgotten in the restaurant, I'd place that single quarter he'd left in the middle of his palm.

"In South Carolina waitresses only make $2.10 an hour before tips."

But, instead of doing what I wanted to do, I stayed inside and cleared their dirty table, wiping away the sticky barbeque sauce they'd spilled beside their plates.

I imagined how things could have been different if Kate and I could have separated things like a centrifuge. If we could have erased certain things we'd done and said to each other from our memory. Could we have talked about kissing, for instance, without both of us thinking about the small bathroom in Georgia where she'd tried to kiss me when she had a boyfriend? I'd told her a year before that night that I would never kiss her again after she'd left me for another guy. She'd walked up to me at the sink and moved in to kiss me, her dress fitting her perfectly. No, I'm getting the timeline confused. That almost-kiss in Georgia wouldn't happen until a year after we sold our plasma. This is the problem with memory—it is not a centrifuge machine, clearly separating one event, one moment from another in our minds.

After a few minutes of being hooked up to the plasmapheresis machine, a yellowish liquid—the plasma and platelets—flowed out of the tube attached to the other side of the centrifuge. The liquid dripped into a clear collection bag. A white foam appeared on top of the yellow liquid, which the clinician assured me was normal.

"Just a reaction to a little air in the centrifuge," she said.

I squeezed the stress ball to encourage continued blood flow. If you don't fill up the whole bag, you don't get paid, the paperwork I signed stated when I'd checked in at the front desk of the clinic.

When Kate and I drove up to the plasma center the first time, the prospect of selling our blood suddenly seemed more than just a questionable idea; it seemed like a scary one. The center, housed in a storefront in a rundown strip-mall, appeared less than sterile, something we could tell from the parking lot.

We'd tried to avoid selling plasma. Kate had taken a second job at a make-up kiosk in the mall—which involved two skills she had that I didn't: applying make-up and sustaining small talk. A friend of mine had hired me to do some administrative work for her real estate business because she felt bad about my current work situation, but, at minimum wage, even two jobs each wasn't enough.

Hearing the machine's pump spin, I started to feel hot and dizzy, but worse than before—my hands clammy around the foam ball, a cold sweat breaking on the back of my neck. I flagged down one of the clinicians and told him I wasn't feeling so well. I pictured a girl I went to college with who went ghost-white after donating blood several years before. When the clinician looked at me, I wondered if he could see the color disappearing from my face, like juice spilling from a glass.

"Here, let's recline your chair a bit. I'll turn down the speed of your machine, too, which should make you feel better." I knew he was trying to help, but what he said only made me feel worse. I tried not to think about the speed of my blood leaving my body, even if slowing it down would help lessen my queasiness. On the side of the off-white plasmapheresis machine a maroon outline of a cheetah was in mid-run. The word "Express" spanned the length of his stride.

The plasma extraction process was less than fast, taking more than an hour for the machine to obtain the amount of plasma needed to fill a bag. The machine worked in cycles. After pulling a certain amount of blood out of my body and separating the plasma and platelets from the red blood cells, the machine stopped drawing blood for a few minutes and pushed cold saline and the plain red blood cells back into my vein—another motion that should have made me feel more at ease during the process (I was getting my blood back!), but instead, I felt sick at the thought of my blood reversing, missing part of what it had when it had first left my body. After several minutes of returning the platelet-less blood back into my arm, the machine turned back on and began pulling more of my blood into the centrifuge to separate.

FDA regulations state that an individual can donate plasma no more than twice every seven days. At fifty dollars a donation, Kate and I could have each potentially made four hundred dollars a month by selling our plasma. Blood money, Kate and I called it.

During one visit my jean shorts rode up and my thighs stuck to the blue pleather recliner. I thought about whether Kate and I were offering ourselves up somehow, giving blood in a strip mall plasma center. Since we were making money, I didn't think it could be called sacrifice, but wasn't sacrifice also the loss incurred by selling yourself at too low a price? I wondered what and how much Kate and I had sacrificed since the night we first kissed our junior year in college. What was the price for the secret we kept?

VARIATIONS ON GRIT

I misremember *Grin and bear it* as *Grit and bear it*.

"Grits take time," my grandmother tells me. "The longer you wait, the better."

Psychologist and researcher Angela Lee Duckworth studies grit.
   "Grit is passion and perseverance," she says in her theory of grit.

In the case of *Grin and bear it*, the *grin* itself, the noun, seems more like *grin* in the 1611 edition of the Bible: a cord or wire, with a running noose, used to catch and hold a wild animal.

In middle school, girls in my town started to wear T-shirts that said "G.R.I.T.S" across the front in cursive letters: Girls Raised in the South. *Grit and Grace*, the words we learned should epitomize women in the South.

Kate teased me for misremembering common phrases like *Grin and bear it*.

She'd say, smiling, "I want to write a children's book with one character whose idioms are always slightly off."

Grit, as a verb, appears in ancient Lithuanian as *grusti*: to crush.

The *whirr, pop!* of a 1917 milling machine grinding corn into grits punctuates the Saturday morning farmer's market in my hometown. *Hominy*, corn hulled and ground into coarse meal. *Hominy*, so close to *homily*, a sermon in church, the words coming out of the priest's mouth.

When someone says that being gay is a sin, I grit my teeth, catch my anger, and hold it there as hard as I can.

Grit, as in to grind or grate your teeth—fear or anxiety or anger turned into sound. Ground into sound.

Every time someone says being gay is a sin, something inside me gets worn down, a stone slowly breaking into sand.

Or, maybe it's not a diminishment but a change of texture. I turn to grit: coarser, rougher.

Or, maybe it's giving me more resolve. More pluck, giving less of a fuck.

In the 1992 movie *My Cousin Vinny*, Vinny Gambini, an inexperienced New York lawyer, goes down South to defend his cousin. Eating breakfast at a small-town, Southern diner, Vinny asks the cook, "What exactly is a grit?"

On my parents' kitchen stove a pot of grits boils. The way my mom cooks them—giving them ample time to simmer—makes them one of the easiest things to eat.

"They taste even better," my mom tells me, "when you cook them with beach water."

Not ocean water, but the tap water at Edisto Beach that's too salty to drink.

Floating perfectly on her back in the ocean, my grandmother told me at the beach one summer that when she got old and she didn't have any teeth, I could just feed her piping-hot grits with a dollop of butter and a dash of salt.

I never told my grandmother that I'm gay. She met Kate, but she never knew I loved her. My grandmother died before I was ready to tell her, before I was ready to tell many people. And throat cancer took her before she lost any of her teeth. Either way, *grin* or *grit*, the mouth is both a site of pain and a site of acceptance.

HOW TO LEAVE

At the end of your childhood, the oaks will not close behind you. The ditches will not dry up completely. The houses in the South have ghosts enough. The swamps have alligators and mosquitoes enough. The back roads have churches and stray dogs enough. The highway shoulders, bones enough.

You can't just leave the South. You must disappear.

First, you must remove certain phrases from your vocabulary. *Y'all* must never leave your mouth. Even though *you guys* isn't quite right, and *you two* or *you four* feel cumbersome in your throat, choose one of these phrases quickly. Think of how you'll greet a crowd before you walk into a room: *Hi, all of you*. Don't drawl the *all*. Say it in a rush.

When you give directions, be more specific than you're accustomed. You will need more than *a ways* when you tell someone how far to go:

1. Give the names of streets
2. Offer an approximate number of miles
3. Do not list trees as landmarks.

Envision a beach without any shells. You will pronounce *conch* strangely when you arrive in California. Not a *conk* on the head. But *consc*iousness. The word will only come up in a conversation about *Lord of the Flies*, about the books you were required to read in school. As a child in South Carolina, you weren't required to read this book. In California, you'll never collect a bucketful of conches at the beach. You will not put them in your windowsill or put one up to your ear to hear *home*.

You will rarely hear thunder, and if you do, you'll forget where you are for a moment. All of a sudden you will be in your childhood bed. Spanish moss will curtain your attic bedroom window, the glass panes fogged with humidity.

It might serve you well to forget cockroaches exist. Where you're going you do not have to worry that they're sleeping in your juice glasses, or crawling under the bed sheets. You realize this is why your mother always corrected you, asked you to put the clean glasses upside-down in the kitchen cabinet, insisted you make your bed every morning. When you turn on your car at night, nothing will scurry away from the shine of your headlights. Nothing will fly towards you like a shadow, all of a sudden alive.

Before you get into your car to drive across the country, put all the tadpoles back. They will not travel well. Carry the large bucket of pond water, where you kept them under the broken-down tree house in your backyard, back to the brick and mortar pond where you caught them as a child. Do not worry if some of them have already become frogs and left when you weren't watching. They have already made it safely down your dirt driveway and back to the same pond where they were born.

When you pour the tadpoles back into the pond, do not give in to the children who stand by and beg you for a few, like coins.

Tell them it is important that they learn how to catch their own. Teach them how:

1. Practice moving slowly. Think of the way sunlight travels across your kitchen floor in the morning. You're eating a bowl of cereal. Your father is in the hall bathroom shaving his face.
2. See the tadpoles sleeping on the pond's algae-covered walls? The algae will be soft and slimy on your hands when you miss and the tadpoles swim toward the bottom.
3. Instead of nets (because you do not have any), you can use a plastic butter container, one of the ones your mother saves instead of buying Tupperware.
4. You must be cautious. Go slowly into the water, like reading words with which you're not yet familiar.
5. Slower. Imagine *circumspect* or *scrupulous*.
6. If you aren't slow enough, and the tadpole wiggles quickly away, do not worry. There will be more time to study them.

You can forget certain spiders, too. Where you're going, spiders will not have legs that look like claws. Or a yellow abdomen, horizontal in its web, stretched wide as a mouth. They will not be named after fruits.

Uncertainty will no longer be in the ocean, but in the ground:

1. Replace e*ye w*ith *epicenter*
2. *Trade winds* with *fault lines*
3. Not *rain bands* but *aftershocks*
4. Not *Beaufort* but *Richter*
5. You will not know destruction by name, but by year. Not *Hugo* but *1989.*
6. You will not wake up in a sweat when your electricity goes out with the wind.
7. But you will wake up wondering whether your bed is shaking, whether the framed picture of your parents is falling off of the wall, whether you're dreaming that the paper lantern hanging from your ceiling is crooked, moving sideways without any wind.

Forget what you know about wisteria. The way the purple climbing vines take over the magnolias in the neighbors' yards each year. The way, as a child, you mistook the dense, delicate orbs for magnolia flowers. Before you knew pretty things could be destructive, could kill a tree if they tried.

Spring will look different where you're going. You won't pick honeysuckle down the path from your parents' house. You won't be able to gauge how far you are into summer by the sweetness of the nectar beading on the pistil you pulled out of the bottom of the tiny yellow-white blooms. Where you're going, the azaleas will be small, and you'll only see them on stands in front of a neighborhood market down the street from your new apartment. The yards won't be pink in March.

Maps will not work the same in California. You will not be able to distinguish where you are in the state by the color or thickness of the dirt. You won't know you're in the northern part of the state by the red clay that stains your knees when you play in your grand-mother's yard. Near the water you won't risk sinking, pluff mud up to your knees.

Let me give you one more thing. Some advice for what you can do during the summer months before you leave: collect teeth.

Sharks' teeth hide in the sand, like they do in a mouth. Remember how the girl you loved in secret slid her tongue into your mouth, grazing the edge of your teeth. How you hid your relationship from your parents, every one of your friends.

You're more likely to find shark teeth near the rock and mortar groins that stretch out into the ocean at high tide, where crabs and fish get trapped when the tide goes back out. Near the rocks your mother told you not to climb as a child. The ones you climbed any-way, careful not to step on the rusty bolts that keep the wooden beams of the groins together.

After college, you work on staff at a summer church camp at the beach. One night after evening chapel you ask the priest, whom you've known since you were in elementary school, whether being gay is wrong. You say you're worried about a friend, hoping he won't suspect anything about you. Sitting with him on the screened-in porch of a beach cabin, you hear the ocean and hundreds of crick-ets rubbing one wing over the teeth of another wing. You wonder if you're grinding your own teeth, if the priest can *hear* your fear, like the rough chirp of all those dune insects.

"Yes," he tells you, "It's not what God intended."

You won't have to be so afraid of kissing a girl where you're going. It will not be a secret you keep. You will learn how to hold a girl's hand in broad daylight, walking down a crowded street.

In the months before you leave, visit small beaches, beaches people from Ohio or Texas or Nevada probably don't know about. Beaches without nearby airports, without blocks of bars and restaurants. Try Edisto. Folly. Or Pawleys Island. Try those small places you can only reach by boat, like Botany Bay and Shute's Folly. Remember how you kayaked to Botany with the girl you loved and filled the bottom of your boats with conch shells the size of a fist, a human heart.

In his old leather wallet your father keeps a bent-edged family photograph of the four of you near one of the rock groins at Edisto. In the photograph, you are five or six, and your brother is two years younger and smiling. You and your brother are both wearing long blue and white pin striped overalls without shirts underneath, like fraternal twins. Your mother has rolled up the legs so they won't get wet in the surf. Neither of you is wearing shoes.

You don't remember this day in particular, but you remember others like it. When you finally tell your parents you're in love with a girl, you worry they'll be disappointed, that they've imagined another life for you. That they imagined a photograph of the kind of life you'd live, of the gender of the person you'd live your life with, that they kept that photograph close to them, maybe without even knowing they had it, without even knowing they were imagining a particular future for you.

Sand sharks can shed 35,000 teeth in a lifetime. Think of the sharp ones in the jewelry box on your bedside table as beads on a rosary. This seems more fitting, a better translation of *rosarium*, more like a crown of roses, a crown of thorns in your hands. Say your prayers by them before bed.

You are not Catholic and have never used a rosary, but you grew up in a church. Pay penance for leaving the church, for wanting to leave the South, for wanting to leave a place you love.

After months of collecting teeth, all of your windowsills in your last apartment in South Carolina will be dangerous with the serrated edges of shark teeth; the chipped bowls you inherited from your grandmother will be full with the sword points and smooth cusps of sand sharks; the delicate, serrated sides of a tiger shark's teeth will circle the candles on your kitchen table; jam jars full of the teeth of lemon sharks will line your fireplace mantle, and the unexpectedly small points of hammerhead teeth will fill the soap dish in the bathroom and sometimes fall into your bath.

But you will not have time for such abundance. In your hand, you'll hold a few sharks' teeth you collected in the months before leaving. The teeth are sharp as certain memories. Think of the girls you loved and lost to boys, religion, a girl's desire for *a normal life*.

Remember how, as a child, noting the strangeness of loss, you rubbed your tongue over the place where a tooth once was, and how a new tooth grew in its place.

BIOGRAPHICAL NOTE

Julia Koets's poetry collection, *Hold Like Owls* (University of South Carolina Press), won the 2011 South Carolina Poetry Book Prize judged by National Book Award Winner Nikky Finney, and her memoir-in-essays, *The Rib Joint*, won the 2017 Red Hen Press Nonfiction Book Award judged by Mark Doty. Her poems and essays have appeared or are forthcoming in *Indiana Review*, *Creative Nonfiction*, and the *Los Angeles Review*. She has an MFA in poetry from the University of South Carolina and a PhD in literature and creative writing from the University of Cincinnati. She currently teaches at the University of South Florida.